How to Lead

When No One Follows

Reversing 25 Years of Failed Political Leadership

In Black America
...Starting with me!

I0094763

How to Lead When No One Follows

By: Jerry L. Maynard, II.

Copyright © 2012 by Jerry L. Maynard, II.

ISBN: 978-0-9826694-8-8

Published by JELAMA Media

With

True Vine Publishing Company

P. O. Box 22448,

Nashville, TN. 37202

www.TrueVinePublishing.org

Printed in the United States of America First Print

Cover design by: Symmetry Media Group

How to Lead
When No One Follows:

Reversing 25 Years of Failed Political Leadership
in Black America
...Starting with me!

Jerry L. Maynard, II

TRUE VINE PUBLISHING CO.

Table of Content

Introduction 11

The Calling 22

Running with the Best of Intentions 34

The People's Choice 50

Have Our Elected Leaders Made a Difference? 63

Remembering a Different Time 77

Change for the Next Generation 91

Reaching the Disaffected 101

The Role of the Business Community in 108

Fostering Partnerships

My Call to Action 119

Conclusion 131

Acknowledgment

I take great pleasure in acknowledging my parents, Bishop Jerry L. Maynard and Pastor Shirley Gaston. Thank you for being an example of servant-leadership. Thank you for training me by taking me to the prisons and homeless shelters to feed the less fortunate and minister to lost souls. I am who I am because of you.

Dedication

This book is dedicated to Mr. Bob Tuke: Thank you for being a warrior for me. I thank God for your mentorship and wise counsel.

Introduction

On November 3, 2008, the voters of the United States elected an African American man to the highest office in the land. President Barack Obama took his oath of office on the mandate given to him by people of every race, gender, religion, and socio-economic background. While support for his candidacy carried across all demographic lines, it was the African American community that galvanized in a way that had not been seen for generations. This new administration was going to mark a change for the black population in our country. We were finally going to have a larger voice in the political process, a seat at the most important table of power, and a greater involvement in the issues of education, business, and justice.

But, the years that have passed since that historic moment have not resulted in the marked change we expected. Instead, much of the African American population has returned to their previous feeling of disconnect toward elected officials and the political system in general. The momentum that was able to create an unprecedented change in 2008 has been stopped short and, even when electing people who come from similar experiences and have reason to share concerns and priorities, African Americans do not trust their leaders. They are not following.

A leader can be defined as someone who is guiding or directing a group of people toward a common goal. The leader of a military unit is in charge of getting his men across the battlefield, and his soldiers trust him with their lives as they follow him into enemy territory. The leader of a band prompts the rest of the musicians to start the song and takes them through every verse until the piece reaches its end; they all need to stay on the same beat and play the same tune or the result will be noise and chaos. We usually think of the quarterback as the leader of a football team, the one who calls the play, makes sure that everyone is positioned before the ball is snapped, and guides his teammates down the field with the common goal of scoring a touchdown. When we reflect on the nature of a leader in the political arena, many of the same characteristics should apply to the men and women who have been charged with directing all of us toward a destination of better schools, safer communities, and more effective and responsive government.

Think about the elected officials who represent you right now. Do you feel as if they are working with you towards a common goal? Do they know what your goals are, or the goals of the community at large? Our councilmen and state legislators and congressmen need to be leading in a way that engages the citizenry and makes us want to march behind them in the battle for our children, our families, our neighborhoods, and our country.

We should want our politicians to come to us and say, "Alright, here's the play that I designed to get us to the next level of economic development and, as a result, to the creation of desperately needed, well-paying jobs. Here's the role I am asking you to play in order to make this goal a reality." We need our politicians—our leaders—to stand with us in front of crowds and demand the change that we need to see in our communities. I wonder how many of us can truly think about leadership in this context and say with conviction that our elected officials are acting as the leaders we need them to be.

I will be examining the lack of true, involved leadership and how the impact of this broken connection is leading to devastating consequences specifically for the African American population. I do not write this as an outsider who has a desire to criticize the system, but as someone who hopes that I am using my leadership positions, both in political and religious circles, as opportunities to engage and involve everyone. I want this book to be a way to examine my own strengths and shortcomings and to start a dialogue with all of you concerning the changes we hope to make together.

The lack of trust among black men and women in our country for the people who represent them is an unfortunate stumbling block to progress in the political system. The suspicion holds true even when the politician who is asking for support is also African American, maybe even more so. When I reflect on the strong African American leadership that paved the way for so many changes in our country—from Harriet Tubman and Frederick Douglass to Martin Luther King, Jr. and Rosa Parks, not to mention the countless leaders in communities whose names we will never see in textbooks—I know that we have a proud history of causing monumental shifts in our society and our laws. African American leadership has proven itself as a key force of progress, but still our communities are not willing to get behind the leaders who are available to us and serving in positions of power here and now.

I will not say that ethnic identity is the dominant factor in determining an African American's decision concerning who to support at the ballot box, because this view diminishes the diverse priorities and interests that exist among African Americans. However, the desire to see more people of color in office is understandably a priority, at least on some level, and this is being accomplished at rates unprecedented since Reconstruction. Why do we have a political structure that now includes more minority representation than any time in history, including a black man who is sitting at the helm of the most powerful office in the world, but yet a population that is apathetic or perhaps even angry when asked to follow these leaders?

I believe that our leaders have not earned the trust of the people who elected them because they rarely returned to the community after taking office. This assertion references back to my earlier definition of leadership. Take a look inside any school, community center, factory, or coffee shop between Labor Day and the first week in November in any election year. You will see dozens of politicians who are doing their best to express sincere interest in the needs of people they are meeting and who stop for every possible photo opportunity.

But, where are these men and women once they have declared victory at the ballot box? How often does your Metro Councilman come back to the elementary school that needed new books and whose students asked him to see the opening performance of their band concert? Did your State Representative ever return to the locally owned restaurant that was in danger of closing due to proposed changes in the tax structure? If our leaders do not come back into the communities and show that they are truly integrated into the concerns and needs of the people, they quickly will discover that, although they may think they are leading, there is no one following.

When we take a detailed look at the statistics over time, we can come to a better understanding of why so many African Americans do not view their leaders as of being capable of, or perhaps even interested in, improving their collective situation. In fact, it is disheartening to realize that as the influence of African Americans has increased in the halls of state legislatures, Congress, and even the White House, the quality of life for African Americans in general has gotten worse. As I will examine in greater detail through the pages of this book, black men and women now claim higher incarceration rates, lower graduation rates, and diminished connection to the vibrancy and improvement in their communities than the period that immediately preceded the great strides made during the Civil Rights movement.

Why has this happened? Why hasn't more official influence resulted in better circumstances for African Americans trying to pay their bills and find their piece of the American dream? A large part of the problem, I contend, is the fact that the people who are now winning elections are many of the same men and women who used to be our community organizers and civic leaders. They have left our neighborhoods with the supposed intention of making a positive change, but all too often leave a vacuum in their wake.

The lack of connection between elected officials and the people who brought them to their positions of elected influence is not entirely their fault. A large part of the problem is simply the nature of bureaucracy and the political system in general. The men and women who go to our city halls and our state houses may do so with the most noble of intentions and actually have constructive ideas that would benefit their communities. They ran for office because they truly wanted to make a positive difference and believed that using the electoral route was the best way to make this possible.

However, it does not take long to discover that affecting change is not as easy as one would hope when you are dealing with lobbyists and financial contributors and other politicians who are eager to strike compromises. The idealism fades, and these leaders who hoped to make a real difference to the people they represent either leave their position or become another participant in the watering down of policies and principles for the purpose of re-election.

Before I lay all of the responsibility at the feet of those who have chosen to lead through elected office, I also want to assert the notion that the citizens who are choosing not to follow have to carry some of the weight for a lack of success in this strained relationship. In order to be clear about the people to whom I am addressing this charge, I first need to share my definition of "followership," because I do not want the term to be tied to a negative connotation.

When someone thinks of a follower, the first inclination might be to envision a weak person who never takes initiative and instead allows someone else to make all of the decisions. This is a person who goes along with the crowd, whether its influence is good or bad. This is not the image of a follower that I want readers to have going forward in this book. Instead, a follower in the political context is a person who is engaged in the process and who has a role that is of equal importance to that of the elected official.

These men and women speak their voices and make their opinions known throughout the community. They are partners in a political relationship that must be healthy and functioning in order for progress to take place. When you think of followers as you digest the thesis and the supporting arguments I present in

this work, please use this framework of people who carefully select, through research and direct interaction when possible, the
leaders with whom they are establishing a cooperative dynamic.
There is no demeaning or lesser intention when discussing the
role of the follower here.

To use an analogy of much greater significance than the
leadership issues I am discussing here, we would do well to remember that Jesus had followers. The disciples were hardly pas-
sive spectators in the ministry of Christ. They were not looked
down upon by others of the faith because they were not the chosen leader. Instead, these men were seen as pillars of strength and
wisdom who's retelling of their time with the Messiah went on to
change the hearts and souls of billions of people.

They were being groomed for the appropriate time to become leaders of other men. When you are asked to be a follower
in a local council race or as a volunteer in the next presidential
election, think about the disciples and what was asked of them.
Followers are vital to a healthy ministry, a thriving business, and
a strong political movement. There is no "lesser than" mentality
here, but an understanding that if each person embraces the role
intended for them, history can be changed. Right now, unfortunately, we do an inadequate job of developing followers to become leaders, and that begins with our inability to gain followers
in the first place. People need to know that every role matters and
has the possibility of changing the social and political landscape.

That being said, those among us who will choose to accept our needed role of followers in the political context must engage in the behaviors and actions needed to make a difference.
Voters should know what their elected officials at the local, state,
and federal level are able to do on their behalf and then demand

that this mission is accomplished. We need to be educated on the roles and restrictions of someone who sits on the Metro Council versus the man or woman who is employed at 1600 Pennsylvania Avenue and make our voices heard accordingly.

Don't expect President Obama to send out a crew to fix a pothole in front of your kid's school, and don't be surprised when the state legislator who represents your neighborhood and several others that surround it tells you that he has scant influence over whether or not we send more troops to Afghanistan. An educated electorate that holds its politicians accountable through dialogue and petition is a powerful tool in the health of our communities.

Look at what happens when citizens are involved and have high expectations for the people they elected. Do you think the neighborhoods with booming economic development, great schools, and roads in excellent condition got that way by chance? Of course not, and there are a whole host of reasons for the disparity between communities, some of which are unfortunately ingrained in our society. However, one factor that can be controlled is regular and strong communication with leaders. We have all heard the term that "the squeaky wheel gets the grease," and in no place is that more true than in politics. When the time comes to advocate for your community, whether the cause be a new playground or more police patrol or a rezoning issue, will you know the place to "squeak," so to speak, to get the attention of the right person? Or, have you become so disconnected from the idea of following any leader that you wouldn't even know where to begin?

Throughout the pages of this book, I will be introducing you to people who represent segments of the African American community and who each have a story to tell that relates to my thesis. You will meet a bus driver who has not received a pay raise in several years and has lost faith that anyone in an official position of power has any real interest in helping her. You will meet a successful entrepreneur who no longer desires to voice his thoughts on political matters through either his campaign contributions or his activism because he sees no difference in the circumstances around him no matter who is elected. You will meet a senior citizen who used to be actively involved in both political and civic issues but has noticed changes over the past couple of decades that have not been for the better and have led to his detachment from the political arena. You will also meet several other men and women who will speak to their lack of confidence in our current leadership. By sharing my ideas and my call to action through these personal stories, I hope that what I am asserting is an idea that you can recognize in your own life as well.

As I explain my thoughts and ideas in the chapters that follow, I want to share that this book began with an examination of my own contributions in the political arena. I spent some serious time questioning if I was still working toward the same goals that I had stated when I first successfully ran for my position on Nashville's Metro Council several years ago and if I was connected enough with my community to know when my efforts were not meeting their needs or priorities. There were several contentious issues that came before our body early in my tenure as a councilman, and I received a crash course in the negotiating and compromising that often occurs when individuals or special interests are anxious for your vote. I was able to see how a politician could enter this arena with the best of intentions and simply become lost in the bureaucracy.

I decided if that ever happened to me, it would be time to leave my position because I could no longer be effective for my constituents. I needed to be able to serve as a leader who was working toward those common goals with the men and women who asked me to represent them. I know that I cannot lead if I am not back in the community on a regular basis—asking questions, observing the environment, and just listening. When I ask people to follow me, I want to make sure I earned the right to expect that following. So, let me be clear in stating that I do not come to you as someone who has figured out the answers, claiming that if you just listen to me our communities will improve and real change will be measured. I instead present myself as both an elected official and a member of the voting community who is eager to improve my own contributions to the political process in hopes of bringing greater opportunity and prosperity for those whom I represent.

As you reach the end of this book, I will offer the same challenge of introspection to you that I have been placing before myself. If you are a person who holds an elected office, I will ask you to think about how connected you are to the community that put you in that position of power and if you realize whether or not people are following. If you are considering a run for office, I will ask you to make the determination right now that you will be both proactive and responsive on behalf of your constituents. And, if you are a citizen who is disillusioned by the lack of understanding or concern that you are seeing from the political system, I hope that you will take some steps to make the leaders more accountable to you and those around you. It will take all of us to reestablish a relationship between leaders and followers that is based on trust, concrete actions and not just promises, and a dedication to the common goal of creating better neighborhoods and a better country for us all.

The Calling

As I will continue to emphasize throughout the book, I do not approach the subject matter as an academic or an analyst who is on the outside of the problem and looking in at what is happening between our elected leaders and their constituents, particularly in the African American community. While the perspective of such researchers certainly has its place in debating my thesis, I offer the voice of someone who has been working in the trenches of political progress and reform for all of my adult life. Even before my active involvement, I was raised in a family that emphasized civic awareness and participation for something greater than one's own advancement. All of my life experiences, from my formal education and my own fights within the political machine as an elected official to my priorities as a father and my responsibilities to lead a congregation from the pulpit, have contributed to my passion for the need to stress and demand real leadership from our politicians. I hope that by taking this time to explain who I am and the familiarity that I have with the leader-follower relationship in many different contexts, I can convey the message that I am promoting on the pages to follow.

I was born in Muncie, Indiana in the 1960s and raised in nearby South Bend. This town is home to the University of Notre Dame as well as several other distinguished colleges and universities. Growing up in an academic town and enjoying regular contact with college students and professors, I quickly developed the sense that serving was an important component of a fulfilling life. The energy of those college campuses, on which ideas for bettering society and protests against injustices were commonplace, inspired me at a young age to be a well-informed citizen from a young age. With that focus in mind, I eventually earned both my Bachelor of Arts and Doctor of Jurisprudence from Indiana University in beautiful Bloomington.

To rewind on my education for a moment, I am blessed that I was told from a young age that I was smart. My parents reinforced the idea that I could do anything and be anything I wanted; there was no limit to my options in life. Knowing that so many children do not receive that encouragement and confidence at home, and being able to look back now and realize how crucial that support was to me, I am drawn to the idea that we need to build one another up and be sources of encouragement, particularly to our young people.

In terms of schooling, the first turning point occurred when I was in the sixth grade. Up until that time, my teachers had always said that I was an average student who would do fine in school but who shouldn't expect too much. Then, I had a teacher by the name of Mr. Goodman who put me in advanced placement courses and told me he believed in me. That was the first time that I had a person of authority, other than my parents, affirmed my intelligence. He changed my life. I went from being a B student to getting As and Bs, and was told by this teacher that those Bs were not good enough. I went from doing enough in school to get by to having a real drive to excel academically. Mr. Goodman served as an early model for true leadership in my life—a man who was committed to knowing the people with whom he was charged to serve and getting the absolute best from them. I wonder if your elected officials know who the "Goodmans" are in their school district. They should.

With the self-confidence to assert my knowledge, I joined the debate team in high school and became its captain during my senior year. I also won a state speech contest that was sponsored by the Rotary Club. Among the sixty or seventy students who competed that year, I was the only black participant. That moment turned my life around, because I realized that I could win in any arena. It wasn't about the color of my skin or any other detail concerning the way I looked; it was about how well I competed. It was disheartening to have several judges share what I assume they thought were compliments with statements like, "I've never heard a black student so articulate" or, "You're different." But, I used those moments to strengthen my determination to prove that intelligent and articulate black men were the norm, not the exception.

When I arrived at Indiana University, there were many African American students on campus and hardly any of us came from what would be considered wealthy families. Most of us were on financial aid or had received a scholarship. Then, I took a road trip to Atlanta with some friends and visited Morehouse and Spelman Colleges. We met African American kids whose parents were doctors and lawyers and judges and congressmen and who had an honored legacy as alumni of the school. I talked with these students, who drove their own BMWs and Mercedes, and they would share stories about vacation spots that I had never dreamed of visiting. I was exposed to this entirely different world in which African Americans were from families that had several generations of wealthy professionals, and I realized that other opportunities could exist for the black community.

While what we learn in textbooks and from intense conversations in both classrooms and dorm hallways are critical to our intellectual and moral development, the basis for my education on all life matters started in my own home. Both of my parents, as well as my grandparents, were in ministry. We visited prisons every month. We fed the hungry every month. My mother worked for the Urban League, offering assistance and support to single moms who were struggling to make ends meet and to create a better future for their kids. It was never a question as to whether we were going to serve our community and be engaged with others in our neighborhood. It was our responsibility to care for one another and know the needs of the men and women around us. It doesn't matter if you are talking about improving life on your street or passing a bill in Congress that will affect the entire country—making change starts here, with concern and a heart of service.

My parents offered me the first two great examples I received about leadership. My mother talked to me about loving myself and also loving others, and that it is always better to give than receive. She taught me to honor others and appreciate the value that every person has to offer the world. My father encouraged me to be tenacious and maximize my potential, never settling for second best. Most importantly, he told me to have faith, no matter what. I have never met a man of stronger faith—faith in God, faith in individuals, faith in the collective human potential. It is because of my father that I refuse to put limits on myself or others. I believe that my parents truly got to the core of what needs to be instilled in any leader—compassion, faith, and a servant's heart—and I am blessed that they were my first teachers and that their handprints are across the work that I strive to accomplish in our communities to this day.

My grandmother always told me growing up that I would be a pastor, but I insisted to her that I was going to practice law. And, I did have a successful career as an attorney that provided me with wonderful experiences and taught me many important lessons about how to lead. In 1993, I began my legal career at Cincinnati's largest law firm, representing a number of Fortune 500 clients in the areas of banking, real estate, health care, construction, commercial lending, and faith-based nonprofit organizations. I joined Nashville's Meharry Medical College in 1996 as the Director of Legal Affairs and Risk Management, serving on the executive leadership team that completed $118 million dollars of capital improvements to the campus. In addition, I served as General Counsel for a private health care center for ten years. I maintain my connection to the legal field as an Adjunct Professor for Fisk University, Meharry Medical College and Tennessee State University teaching Health Law, Business Law and Ethics. My time in both the private and public sectors, and specifically working in the fields of education and healthcare, was invaluable in developing an in-depth understanding of how one can easily get lost in bureaucracy and forget the cause or the people for whom he is fighting.

Grandma was also right, though, and my family lineage proved to be an indication of where I would land. I grew up in church, attending some form of service five days a week. Monday night was Bible study, Tuesday was church service, Wednesday was choir rehearsal, Thursday was the children's ministry, and Friday brought another church service. Then, of course, on Sundays we had Sunday school and two more services to attend. I knocked on doors witnessing from a young age and grew up immersed in service. More importantly than anything family history could provide, I received a calling from the Lord that set me on my current path. I accepted my appointment as Senior Pastor for Southside Community Church in 2008. I am now a fourth-generation pastor, and my work in this capacity has taught me some of my most important lessons about being an effective leader. That education started with learning how to be a follower.

I had to follow in the footsteps of my father, who was the senior pastor at our church, for twelve years before stepping out on my own. I was engaged in every part of the process, from welcoming guests to helping with the development of sermons to cleaning up the pews after the service. Waiting for my turn at the pulpit did not mean just sitting with the congregation and hoping that my moment would arrive soon. My father knew that I had lessons to learn as an active follower before I would be ready to ask others to join as partners in my leadership efforts. I will admit, this role of follower was a difficult one for me to accept. I thought I was ready to be a pastor five years before my dad finally decided that my time to lead had come. Looking back now, I am grateful for my father's wisdom in knowing that I was not yet in a position to lead. There must first be an appetite to follow, to be engaged in the environment and anxious to learn and absorb as much as possible.

No matter the context, be it within a church congregation, a Fortune 500 company, or in the political arena, we must serve in the important role of follower, or apprentice, before we consider taking another step forward. Think about the head football coaches in the National Football League. You would be hard pressed to find one who did not take the field as a player at some point in his career, or perhaps even as a member of practice squad before making the starting line-up. There was a time when even the great Patriots coach Bill Belichick had to listen to someone else and learn to excel in different aspects of being a follower. Without that experience and ability to relate to all facets of the team dynamic, I don't think he would have those Super Bowl rings. Similarly, I would not be able to lead and meet the needs of my congregation if I had not listened to my father and prepared myself for the time when I would be able offer my service most effectively.

In addition to doing my best to provide leadership from the pulpit, I have seen the amazing changes that can come from the political arena when engaged leaders are in place and for years I have worked to make my voice part of this system. In South Bend, we had a mayor, a congressman, and a dominant number of city councilmen who were affiliated with the Democratic Party. I witnessed the ways in which the government could create an environment in which all people could live and succeed. I took the message and platform of the Democrats to heart and have been engaged in the process for years.

In 2004, I served as the Tennessee Outreach Director for Senator John Kerry's Presidential campaign, and the following year I was selected to serve as the Deputy Chairman of the Tennessee Democratic Party under Chairman Bob Tuke, in which position in which I was responsible for the Party's day-to-day operations. In 2006, I served as the Tennessee Outreach Coordinator for Congressman Harold Ford, Jr.'s campaign for the United States Senate and was elected to the Tennessee Democratic Executive Committee for Senate District 19. I was honored to be elected to serve on the Democratic National Committee's Standing Committee on Credentials representing President-Elect Barak Obama in 2008.

While proud of the work I was able to do in each of my administrative roles, I knew that I needed to make a difference by offering my name as a candidate for an at-large seat on Nashville's Metro Council in 2007. I saw that in our community, there were many people who did not have a voice, many people who were left out because of special interests. The powerful and the rich seemed to be getting the attention of the government. I saw that there were areas of Nashville that were ignored and not receiving any investment. The schools in certain areas of town were not functioning at a high level, and the students were not getting the education they needed and deserved. I noticed that jobs were being created disproportionately in certain communities, while other neighborhoods struggled with paralyzing unemployment. Housing was dilapidated in pockets of Nashville, and there were areas of ghettos and hopelessness.

I decided to run for office because I wanted to make sure that all Nashvillians, no matter where they live, have the opportunity to live the American dream. I thought that I could make a difference representing not only people who don't have a powerful voice right now in our government, but also by advocating policies and priorities that would lead to the betterment of all Nashvillians. I am pleased that in 2011 the voters of Nashville deemed my efforts on their behalf worthy of four more years in office, as I was reelected to serve a second term in my position. I plan to keep improving in my role as leader and do my best to make myself worthy of the relationship that my constituents have asked me to continue with them.

My experiences serving on prominent committees for the Democratic Party and the past four years I spent working for the people of Nashville on the Metro Council have intensified my passion for encouraging true leadership and putting a highlighted focus on instances in which the relationship between leader and follower is not working. I have been a part of too many discussions that consider the needs of financial supporters, lobbyists, and other government officials, but not the constituents we have been given the honor of serving. I have learned that you will not be an effective and transforming leader just by listening to whoever happens to be the loudest. You must know what is in the best interest of the entire community, and that can be accomplished only by taking a step back from the bureaucratic mess and returning to the neighborhoods, the schools, and the businesses. Leaders must be ready to listen.

I am writing this book because I am committed to making political leaders, myself included, more accountable to the communities they serve. We cannot lose sight of the reasons we were elected, one of which certainly was not to take carefully measured steps that will benefit our own self-interest in getting re-elected. I have to admit that it is easy to develop tunnel vision and see only the people who are the inside players in politics if you do not step out of that environment. You will lose sight of the needs of the people, the desires of the people, and the pains and struggles of the people. I want to remind my fellow politicians that the only way to serve the community is to be in the community. And, that doesn't mean just holding town hall meetings and inviting people to come to you. You need to go into people's homes and supermarkets and places of worship. Go to where the people are and then learn from them. Don't campaign; just communicate.

There are leaders who have served or are currently serving the people wonderfully, and I will ask you to think of them as examples of politics being done right as you read through the pages of this book and learn more about my proposals for change. I use their careers as models for my pursuit of effective leadership. President Barack Obama is our best and most prominent example of a politician doing it right. While his opponents may scoff at his background as a community organizer, I believe it is exactly this experience that keeps our president connected to the needs of the people in this country. He spent decades in challenging neighborhoods and produced a track record of working with everyday citizens around him to improve schools, job growth, and community pride. He displayed a powerful confidence and sense of audacity, as the title to one of his books puts it, to believe that he could run for the presidency after serving not even one full term as a member of the political bureaucracy. Why not? His determination to be at the forefront of change is incredible; he is incredible. And, as I publish this book, our President is only a few days away from Election Day and the culmination of a close, tough, and very personal campaign season. His success at the polls will depend in no insignificant way to the mobilization of the African American vote. Will black men and women support President Barack Obama with the enthusiasm and sheer numbers that they did four years ago? If they do not, will their lack of involvement contribute to a political shift that will alter the fundamental path for our country? Many of you reading this book already know the answers to these questions. For me, at this moment, these are issues that weigh heavily on my mind as I lay out my thesis on the pages before you.

My dedication to the continued success of our president stems in part from the fact that it is difficult for me to provide any other outstanding examples of political leadership in office today. I have to reach back at least ten or twenty years to find names of politicians who had a real impact on me. These men include the late Harold Washington, who served as mayor of Chicago for four years in the mid-1980s, and Maynard Jackson, who was the first African American mayor of Atlanta and held that position from 1974 to 1982 and again from 1990 to 1994. Also, I have great admiration for Congressman John Lewis, not so much for his work in the House of Representatives, although I do respect his voting record there, but for the courage he showed as a leader in the civil rights movement. He was a young man, only a student at the time, but felt the conviction to take a stand in a way that directly impacted millions of lives. All three of these leaders opened doors in government and areas of our society for so many who followed them. I truly believe you cannot have a great nation when a segment of the population is disenfranchised, ignored, powerless, and without hope. In these aspects and so many others, these men have effected positive change.

Beyond the world of elected leaders, Thurgood Marshall is my hero. He serves as an inspiration to many and should be studied as a model of leadership for anyone who wants to make a real difference. While an attorney for the NAACP, Marshall traveled to cities both in the North and South to confront segregation and racism. Even though he faced threats to his life in every place he visited, he relentlessly fought against the injustices faced by African Americans. Marshall eventually became one of the most brilliant Supreme Court justices we have ever had. Thurgood Marshall understood the fact that you could not have a nation which garnered pride as long as so many people who lived within its borders suffer from brutality and indignation based on the color of their skin or their socioeconomic status. He advocated the idea that the Constitution is a living, breathing document that must be applied to each individual situation and be used in a way that would administer the law equitably to all.

So, these professional background and life experiences are the foundation for the points that I will emphasize throughout this book. I have worked as an attorney who has had to negotiate with the lobbyists and the doctors and the politicians to get people the health care that they deserved. I have stood in front of a congregation and asked the members of my church to come with me on a journey that will bring each one of us a closer relationship with God and provide the opportunity to offer service to anyone in need. I have sat in Metro Council meetings and confronted the frustration that stems from bureaucratic red tape when all I wanted to do was help bring a better life to the people I was charged to serve. I have talked to our elders who say that civic engagement and activism just isn't like it used to be and to teen-agers who could not care less about our government and see no need to take part in the political process. I recognize the disconnect that has been growing between our elected officials and their constituents, and I want to make my voice heard and then join with you in making changes.

Running with the Best of Intentions

I have had the pleasure and honor of serving in several capacities within the world of politics, from holding the title of Deputy Chairman of the Tennessee Democratic Party to my current position as Councilman At-large with the Metropolitan Government for Nashville & Davidson County, and through these roles I have met some fabulous men and women who pursued their seats as elected officials with intentions that were noble and in the best interest of the community. These were not politicians who put their name on the ballot because the family business was politics and holding office was simply what they were expected to do or because they hoped to achieve fame and power, but because they truly had the hearts of servants. It was usually one specific issue that propelled them to action, such as education or road construction, and from that seed of activism a true leader was born.

I like to think that I fit into the category of political figures who entered into the arena for the right reasons. I am passionate about my hometown of Nashville and I hope that I am able to play some small role in improving the lives of people who live here and also create a welcoming city for others who want to come and make it their home. I had already spent many years in politics when I decided to take on the role of candidate, so I was hardly naïve about the process when I won my first county-wide race in 2007. I knew that I would not show up for my first council meeting, propose some legislation, and produce high-paying jobs, quality health care, and safer schools for our children by the time I left for home at the end of the night. Getting most things accomplished within a political context requires negotiation, persuasion, and networking. You just need to be careful not to lose yourself in the process.

Let's start by taking a look at how well-intended people end up in political office, and then try to learn how they can avoid the pitfalls that tend to engulf us in public office. There are many individuals who serve as community leaders and activists, and they do so not because of the title but because of their interest in making a difference in the neighborhoods or the cities in which they live. Many of these activists, as I mentioned earlier, focus on one or two policy items, such as crime, the environment, education, or healthcare. Or, their involvement could be prompted by a single act, such as the installation of a trash dump in their community. These men and women, most of whom never dreamed of being political players, are now private citizens who reach out to elected officials on behalf of their community and neighbors.

When I moved to Nashville in 1995, I immediately noticed the lack of economic development and job creation in the urban core areas of our city. I also realized that our local government failed to include female-owned and minority businesses in the awarding of government contracts. With the rich history of the civil rights movement in Nashville and the colleges and universities in the city, I did not understand how our city's leaders allowed such great disparity when it came to jobs, public investment and the procurement of contracts. These issues collectively became my cause and I began a crusade to challenge the Mayor and our Metro Council to make investments in our urban core, redevelop our blighted neighborhoods and award lucrative contracts to companies that had been historically locked out.

For eight years I advocated for disparity studies and remedies for past business discrimination, served on information panels, wrote op-eds, gave interviews and organized town hall meetings to deal with the inequality of economic development in urban Nashville and the disenfranchisement of our minority businesses.

Like others, after years of trying to make a difference on a specific issue as a private citizen, the point may come when a community activist realizes she needs greater access to those who seem to have the real influence over what gets done. It stands to reason that endless pounding on a politician's door for just five minutes of attention may make a person wish he was on the other side of that exchange. He decides to become part of the government that he feels was either unresponsive or even created the problem in the first place. They intend to achieve a greater position of power in order to accomplish the desired change. The motives are genuine. How many of us have had that moment when we looked at a politician going on endlessly and coming through our television screens and thought to ourselves, "Give me his job for a week. I'd fix this mess." It's when a novice leader takes that quiet challenge to the next level and actually puts his name on a ballot that a crash course in political games becomes inevitable.

Some people run because they believe that taxes are too high or government is too big, and so they hope to use their position to take steps that will reduce the size and scope of government. Others feel that their school system is failing their children; they run to provide more funding to public schools or to advocate for the growth of charter school options or to pass measures that will make it easier for parents to choose the option to home school. Whatever the policy issue may be, these activists approach the topic with laser beam focus and with proven knowledge of the people and the facts involved. And, because of this developed level of respect, these men and women often will have a built-in base of supportive followers who are ready to work for them as candidates and believe they can effect real change in the halls of government. How often, it is sad to say, the results we seek are harder to come by once we leave the role as activist to politician. Make no mistake—as I've said before, I count myself among the guilty at times when it comes to not satisfying my constituents. Of course, you will never be able to make everyone happy. I am hoping, though, that at least shedding some light on the realities of our office duties and sharing my perspective as one person who struggles to meet expectations will spark some dialogue between leaders and followers about how we can best move forward together.

Here's the truth facing a first-time political leader. After we have completed our run for office and been elected, what we sometimes don't realize is the mechanisms of the position we now hold. We cannot focus simply on the issue or that particular matter on which we ran. We have to be ready to address issues about which we had been largely unfamiliar before earning a seat of power. As much as we may want to put all of our attention toward the policy for which we have so much passion, this single-mindedness is not realistic. With this realization in mind, some politicians may become overwhelmed by the daunting task of maneuvering through the elected body of which they are now members. Whether it's the local city council, Congress, your state assembly, the governor's office, or other political arenas, there is a protocol and procedure to be followed. The situation becomes even trickier when you realize that some of the rules by which you must now play are unwritten. There is both an art and a science to working in government that you can learn how to operate only with on-the-job training and this learning experience can leave idealists quite jaded. When you take your seat in chambers with the enthusiastic intention of sending that garbage dump facility out of your district right away, and eight months later you have spent all of your time arguing over the city budget, frustration sets in.

In 2007, I ran for office on a four prong political platform that included 1. economic development & job creation in the urban core; 2. more affordable housing development for working families; 3. equality and fairness for all Nashvillians; and 4. fully funding our public schools. After a successful campaign and my perceived mandate from the citizens of Nashville, I went to work in the Metro Council on day one to fulfill my campaign promises. Little did I know that our government was structured in a way that the Mayor had most of the power and the Metro Council could not initiate and pass certain types of legislation that would cost money without the approval of the Mayor's Office. This was not Congress with the legislature sharing power with the Executive Branch equally. The authors of our Metro Charter intentionally created a government with a strong Mayor and weak legislative branch.

Needless to say, I had a rude awakening when I offered legislation and other progressive initiatives for consideration, only to be told that the Metro Council did not have the authority to create the changes I desired.

So, how do we navigate through these new waters of elected office? Many of us hire consultants when we are trying to earn votes. We carefully select a campaign manager and may hire a public relations specialist as well. For those with the funding and the hopes of a position that requires speeches in front of crowds, we also may bring a speechwriter on board as part of the team. But how many of us have ever hired a consultant to help us become a better legislator? Once we are elected, most politicians have a huge learning curve. But there is now no one around to groom us, to train us, to teach us, to consult with us on how to become an effective elected official. We are left with a lot of questions about how to approach both the legislative agenda and our constituents. This factor is key when dealing with constituents who easily become critical of, and cynical toward, their elected officials. The reality is, at least for a while, we are not as polished and effective as we may have appeared while enjoying the assistance of our campaign team, and we need time to establish some traction.

Somehow, if we make an effort, our adeptness at handling the job should develop over time. In most instances, we discover the nuances of the position on our own. But, what do we lose during the time we need to work through the learning curve? By the time that we come to the end of our initial terms, four years or two years, and it is time to reach out to the voters again, we will find some constituents who are unimpressed with our service, and unhappy with our performance. While we may believe that we have been correctly focused on learning to do our job well, the impression to the public is that we did not deliver on the matters we promised to change.

Such was the case with my first year as an elected official. Working with the Mayor and North Nashville community, Nashville was successful in obtaining a beautification grant totaling nearly a million dollars to beautify a blighted urban area. This had never been accomplished before and I was proud that a historic corridor in urban Nashville that had fallen into disrepair was going to receive nearly a million dollars in beautification. However, three years later, not one flower, tree or shrub had been planted for the project because of federal and state government red tape.

Many members of the community felt that I had failed to deliver after announcing to the community that I had made good on my campaign promise "of public investment in the urban core to help blighted neighborhoods." In three years, nothing had changed. We received the grant, but the project was stalled for three years as we worked through the government maze. I was told projects that involve multiple government agencies at the federal and the state level sometimes take three to ten years to complete. This was my "on the job training" and my constituents were not impressed.

Another issue to consider is that there are often elected officials with more seniority and experience who will take advantage of the fact that there are novice politicians in their midst. It is not unheard of for those persons who have been in office for a significant length of time simply to tell the freshman politicians to go and sit down somewhere so that the adults can do the business of the government without the neophytes getting in the way. They take advantage of the inexperience of the newly elected officials, who are usually more than willing to stand on the sidelines as they struggle to digest all that must be learned about their new job. This inaction, of course, does not help the constituents grow any faith in their leaders. This situation is a byproduct of a complicated system that finds multiple ways to put boundaries, both real and assumed, between political leaders and their followers. Knowing this fact, I reached out to several veteran elected officials to seek their wisdom and advice right after my 2007 election. There were two council persons that had been around government as elected officials or public service employees for more than twenty years who agreed to offer wisdom. I sat down with them and absorbed their wisdom, history lessons and experiences like a sponge. The more I listened, the more they offered. But, there were others who had their own agendas. They offered information that was tainted with their self-interests and self-serving motives. One veteran councilman told me point blank that the Council was made up of forty jealous whores. When I asked him to explain, he said that he was unwilling to give me what had taken him more than fifteen years to acquire—knowledge.

So who do you trust as a newly elected official? With all of the problems and issues facing urban Nashville, I didn't have four years to learn the system. I had a zeal and passion to affect change now. However, I didn't have the knowledge to understand how to make that change in the political system of which I now was a part. I had been heavily involved in council matters and followed legislation as a community activist. I had worked with government officials to get things done in my community. But, now, I was the one who had to take the community's desires and properly navigate the government and political systems while combating my adversaries who held opposite positions to mine. Every day I told myself that I would not be an elected official who was satisfied with the title only. I wanted to change my community effectively for the better. So, with this task at hand and little experience as a councilman, I decided on my game plan: Lead, Fight & Make Mistakes.

The time had come for me to decide if I wanted to be loved by everyone, take few risks and avoid the possibility of failure . . . or fight for what I believed in, aware that I didn't have all of the tools and knowledge to win every battle. I chose to fight and learn.

It also is important to keep in mind that there are few offices to which you can be elected that will not have someone else dictating the policy agenda, at least to some degree. The mayor, governor, and president come to their offices with clear objectives in mind, and will use their power and persuasion to guide the work of the legislature. With the rare exception of leadership positions in the legislative branch, your office has you at the mercy of what other politicians deem important. You certainly can get to know the right people and become a trusted advisor in their eyes so that your policy priorities earn some clout, and you always should continue to push for the measures that will help your community, no matter how small others may find your voice, but be prepared to fight for any and everything you try to accomplish no matter its nobility.

So, there you are as a newly elected official with the best of intentions and plans to do important business on behalf of the people who elected you. What many of us find is that the system of government moves at a pace and in a way that consumes the most ambitious leader. You are dealing with government bureaucracy, agendas of the executive branch, special interests, and other advocacy groups that carry a large figurative bullhorn. You must then also tackle the day-to-day operations of political life, which are not nearly as glamorous or dramatic as they appear in prime-time television dramas. Most locally elected officials are the front line for constituent services. Plus, most voters demand and expect to talk directly with their elected officials. This means meetings. In the Metro Council I have heard more than twenty council persons say they didn't know the job consumed this much time and required so many meetings and a heavy work load. Quite honestly, I have seen some of my colleagues overwhelmed by community and constituent meetings that it dampened the spirit with which they entered the office in the first place. What can happen next is an attempt by a frustrated or lazy elected official to legislate while avoiding the interference of constituent meetings. What results is the disconnect that forms the central theme and concern of this book.

At some point, members of the community that elected you to office are going to realize that are not able to focus on your preferred issues or deliver all of the campaign promises for which you were sent to serve in the first place. While you may be frustrated with the multiple diversions and tendency toward inaction, the disappointment of voters is likely multiplied because they are not privy to the reasons discussed above. Some feel betrayed because you voted on a matter in support of a colleague or to please the mayor and your stance on the issue not to their liking. They may not be fully informed that the vote was necessary in order to get political support for your community's list of priorities.

I have seen voters express to politicians that they have been hoodwinked. Voters sent you to your elected position with a specific issue in mind, with a specific agenda, and now they feel that you are simply a rubber stamp for the executive branch or the caucus of the political party to which you belong. As a result, some people in the community will stop following and will stop listening to you because you as an elected official cannot have an intense focus on the issues for which you fought with such determination as a private citizen and activist. It is true—we sometimes give the impression that other issues are more important to us than those that matter to the community. Whether or not that is entirely fair given the nature of our work, this impression can remain. I know because I have been there; I see the legitimate frustrations from both sides of the relationship.

I came to office focused on the issues on which I ran. But, the first major piece of legislation the Metro Council had before it was the extension of a sports arena lease agreement with our professional hockey team and additional money from our government to subsidize the privately owned hockey team's operation. I did not run for office to give more government money to millionaires so that they could avoid financial losses in the operation of their business. However, this matter was critical to the economic sustainability of our downtown. If the hockey team moved, we faced economic hardship with the closing of restaurants, bars, the loss of sales tax revenue and Nashville owning a big empty arena.

After the Mayor introduced legislation to extend the hockey team's lease and increase the government subsidy to the team, several community organizations expressed their opposition to giving more money for sports while our schools needed more resources. I found myself in a tough position. My constituents demanded that I focus on the issues they sent me to tackle such as affordable housing, job creation and public education. But, I could not ignore my duty of due diligence to determine if losing the hockey team would be detrimental to our city. I will never forget a community meeting I attended while this debate to pass the Mayor's initiative was in full swing. A pastor stood up and asked me, "Are you going to be another politician in the good ole boy system where the rich and powerful get richer and more powerful while our community gets nothing?"

His question was bruising to say the least. I had worked so hard for so many years to make my community better and now within months of being elected, my personal commitment to it was being challenged. Our relationship with voters is just like any other relationship we value in one very important aspect— communication is the most important element. The task of staying in touch with the men and women in your district may seem cumbersome given all of the other time-consuming responsibilities of your new position, but it is as least as crucial now as when you were running for office. This needed focus on personal communication is especially true for part-time elected officials, usually those at the local level. When you are working for a city council, the staff and resources are limited. You probably do not have someone to answer your mail or even take your phone calls most of the time. In such situations, the government has intentionally created smaller districts so that elected officials and their constituents can interact directly without barriers. While this responsiveness sounds wonderful and responsive in theory, the challenge is that most part-time politicians also work full-time jobs and have family responsibilities. And, if you are a good legislator, you quickly will discover that the hours you dedicate to the elected office hardly constitute part-time work. You can practically get buried in all of the responsibilities of reading legislation, attending community and political meetings, going to ceremonies, answering constituent correspondence, and, of course, dealing with the business of the government.

Take, for example, the Metro Council in Nashville on which I currently serve. Our staff is limited, our budget has been cut by 26% over the last four years, and we are paid $13,000 a year. We don't have anyone to answer mail or help with e-mails or complete research on our limited budget. The resources simply are not there, and you quickly can become overwhelmed. I can tell you from personal experience, as someone for whom it is imperative that I represent my constituents well and remain as accessible as possible, it literally can feel like an avalanche is coming down around me as I struggle to meet my obligations. If my response to a voter's email takes longer than I would like, or I don't respond at all, that person is going to think that I am just another politician who doesn't care about the needs of the people. I assure you this is not the case.

Whether or not it is fair, some of your constituents will come to think that you are unresponsive and uncaring about their needs simply because there are not enough hours in the day to handle this important job by yourself. And, most likely, you will be doing it mostly by yourself. So, I took a deep breath after hearing the pastor's question. I exhaled and responded that hockey deal was not one of my priorities. But, after looking into the matter, it was important to my community to extend the lease because people in my community would lose jobs downtown if the hockey team left town. This issue of jobs was my priority. I then informed the group of two important pieces of legislation that dealt with healthcare and contracts for minority business that I had signed and filed and the timeline within which they would be passed.

As the group listened, I spoke from my heart and said, "Our community has suffered from these issues for over twenty years. I just elected within the past six months. Give me a chance to make a difference. I promise I will serve and lead." The group applauded and I learned an important lesson in what an amazing difference just a few moments of honest dialogue can make.

I am not sharing this information to complain about my workload or gripe about how hard it is to be an elected official. I feel honored to have been given the opportunity to serve, and it is not a charge that I take lightly. I know that I am blessed to represent the people of Nashville as we work to make our great city even better. However, I want to express the fact that it is easy to get caught up in the mundane tasks of office, because those obligations must be met, and I want voters to know that for most of us this struggle is one we work to reconcile throughout our political careers.

I have dear colleagues in the Metro Council who approached the challenge of elected office in order to tackle a specific issue. They were really motivated and thought they could make a difference in their community. This drive and determination is admirable. But, when these well-intentioned men and women got caught up in the bureaucracy that sometimes dominated local government and their key issues were put on hold, it is at this time that communication with constituents was essential. Voters need to know that we have not forgotten why we were elected. Give them enough credit and respect to explain the process and the challenges you are facing. Throughout our history, the American people have shown themselves to be forgiving when leaders are upfront and honest. I can just imagine the power of a community meeting in which an elected official sits down with those in his neighborhood and admits that he did not anticipate all of the bureaucratic and administrative hurdles that are a part of the job. That moment of honesty would probably go further in building relationships with constituents than any staged campaign event. The voters don't want us to be perfect and have everything figured out; they want us to be accessible and willing to work hard on their behalf. Let's bring them into this process and share the roadblocks that are faced on a weekly basis, not to make excuses but to offer transparency and a desire to bring our followers into the fold as much as possible.

It would be interesting to take a poll of elected officials at all levels of government to find out their reasons for getting into politics. Do they still remember that one issue that propelled them to action? Can they still take themselves back to that first school board meeting that they attended as a concerned parent, when they realized that they needed to be a bigger part of the change our kids deserved? I wonder if some of these leaders do not allow themselves to think about that passion and drive they once held, because the reality of the governmental bureaucracy has created a much different reality in which they must now live. After a legislative session that was spent fighting about one sentence in an eighty-page bill, it is difficult to maintain the momentum to fight for their issues. The inflated sense of power that they felt on the evening that the voters chose them as representatives has been diminished by the need to adapt to the agendas of others, the sometimes ugly deals that that are brokered in back rooms that compromise their values and priorities, and simply the volume of work under which they are now buried. We as elected officials perhaps *should* take a moment to think about why we first felt the desire to run for office as a way to shed some of these damaging effects of life in government and get back to the pure connection we once had with our constituents. If this mental exercise is done regularly, we have a chance of reconnecting our leaders with our followers. Then, we can work together to do the business of the people with those original and community-focused intentions in mind.

The People's Choice

You often will hear people offering a correction to those who say that we live in a democracy, putting forth the reminder that our country was instead founded as a republic. This means that we do not vote on every issue directly, but select a group of men and women who we entrust to represent our interests in positions of political power. In a nation of millions, this system was preferred to the undertaking needed to gather the vote of every eligible person. Can you imagine the entire population of the state of Tennessee (or at least those who choose to be involved) gathering in the State Capitol every time we needed to make a decision about taxes, education, or an emotional hot-button issue like abortion or marriage? The halls would be a bit crowded to say the least. So, we go to the ballot box at regularly scheduled intervals and choose people to make those difficult decisions on our behalf. How often, though, have you supported a candidate and felt confident that he would advocate for the issues that mattered to you only to discover that your voice meant nothing after Election Day? What is the responsibility, if any, of our elected leaders to vote according to the people's will once in office? I argue that if this will is being ignored, you will find an electorate that becomes disengaged and disillusioned.

As I spend my time reaching out to voters, both when I was running as a candidate and also in my capacity as a council person, I have heard time and again from voters who feel like their local elected officials do not vote in accordance with the interests and desires of their constituents. These voters attended community meetings and public forums when a contentious issue arose and let their representative know how they felt on the matter, only to have the official vote contrary to their position. It's not surprising to learn that so many men and women in our community have reached the conclusion that their voice is irrelevant in the political process. If you are a politician who makes it clear that you want members of your community around only when it's time to vote but would rather not hear from them any other time of year, or at least if you do hear from them, it won't change how you vote, then you are not going to find people following you for very long.

We see the result of an electorate losing faith in the idea that politicians might actually listen to them whenever an election rolls around for offices such as mayor and school board. I'm amazed when I review the results of these local contests, especially those that do not have the benefit of an accompanying state or federal election, and see that only four or five hundred people voted in a district that contains 16,000 potential voters. It's a problem that continues to grow and build momentum—politicians don't listen, so the voters stop trying to be heard; voters aren't speaking out leading up to and during elections, so politicians don't think it is worth their time to listen. What will it take to make this pattern end and instead create a system in which our leaders are responsible to the needs of their constituents and the voters are engaged to make sure this relationship is maintained?

In most countries in which free elections are held and participation is encouraged, the voter turnout rate stands at between eighty and eighty-five percent. It is just understood in these places that you are going to exercise your right to vote. In 2008, when President Barack Obama was elected, the pundits in our country were thrilled over the fact that 64% of eligible voters cast a ballot. Of those who were voting in an election for the first time, 40% of them were black men and women. We had not seen that high a percentage of voters come out for a presidential election in a century. And, the number of people who voted, 130 million, was the highest in history. Even though the numbers still weren't impressive in comparison to other nations, some of us hoped that the 2008 election would mark a turning point in electoral politics and we would see a shift to greater involvement by all people, and particularly those who had long been underrepresented.

The excitement that surrounded the Obama campaign several years ago does not seem to have carried over into subsequent elections. The midterm elections that were held in 2010 brought out around 42% of eligible voters, which marked just a one percent increase over the midterm elections that were held four years previously. This decreased participation affects all of the state and local elections that ride on the coattails of federal races, such as those for governor and members of state legislatures. While elections for president get a great deal of media attention and bring out the volunteers, it is often these state and local elections that directly affect a community's quality of life in areas concerning education, employment, and crime. The absence of each voter is felt so acutely when we are deciding on the candidates who will best represent our needs in these elected offices.

And, as I mentioned earlier in the chapter, the lack of engagement at the local level is even more pronounced. In my city of Nashville, the elections in 2011 to elect our mayor and fill forty seats on the Metro Council brought out just less than 24% of eligible voters. School board elections, which have a tremendous impact on the quality of education that our children receive in our city, as well as school reform, teacher training programs, and after school activities, usually do not even draw half of the meager turnout that the mayoral races receive. We allow only a few hundred voices in each district determine the fate of 79,000 children for the thirty-five hours they spend in our schools every week. What is it about the process that is making us not want to share our voice or believe that it won't be heard no matter what we do?

The reality is that people are now making their voices heard by not voting. They are sending us a message by staying home. The statement being made is, "I've looked at the people who are running and I don't see a hint of difference between any of you. You've shown me that my vote means nothing so why waste my time?" Part of this disenchantment is rooted in a real lack of service on the part of elected officials, but lack of communication is also a contributing factor here. Yes, it's true that in too many instances we have failed as politicians and the supposed leaders of our communities to be advocates for people in a way that really matters. We have let the mundane details of the office bog us down or, equally as negative, we have become consumed with the trappings of power and turned to unveiling what the position can do to advance us personally and professionally. There is no doubt that the citizens' lack of faith in the system has a legitimate foundation. But, what about the instances in which men and women on the city council or in the state legislature are working for the will of the people but that message still isn't being heard. We need to do a better job of communicating with our constituents about what is happening in our offices so they see that voting truly does make a difference. Despite those who cling to the notion that circumstances won't change no matter who is in office, I hold firm to the idea that voting is the cornerstone of our country and the best way to ensure justice for our people does progress.

African Americans cannot afford not to be involved in the political process because we are disproportionately affected by every difficulty that our country faces. Just look at unemployment numbers or health concerns or home foreclosures or urban decay—the black population in the United States continues to face more severe consequences in every one of these areas. Have we reached the point of throwing our hands up and simply accepting the fate of a people who bear the brunt of society's ills, or are we going to fight to choose elected officials who will take the status quo to task and push for real change?

It is understandable that voters will become cynical and detached when they believe that their elected officials are voting contrary to their district's interest. But, if the politicians are not listening to their constituents, who is instead receiving their attention when they are deciding how to vote on a particular issue? We must discuss the reality that sometimes a person was not elected to represent all of the people in his or her district, but rather hand-picked by a few people who activate the voters they want with the intention of having this politician in place to do their bidding. There may be an advocacy group or people representing a special interest who are driven to political involvement by a specific issue and seek out the candidates who will vote correctly on any measure dealing with this issue. Or, this well-organized group simply may not like the incumbent currently holding an office and therefore use the strength of its numbers and resources to get another leader in that job instead. In local elections with fewer than a thousand people casting a ballot, the influence of a labor union or a business interest or a concerned group of citizens is more than substantial. Perhaps it really is just these groups that are determining who holds our seats of power, and there is no choice made by the people after all.

Let's look more closely at the way in which a special interest group can hand-pick a candidate and then go on to dictate this person's entire voting behavior once elected. It is not uncommon for a group to interview candidates for a political position in order to determine who it will support in an upcoming election. Or, if there is a person in the community who may never have entertained the idea of seeking public office but who stands for the values or the priorities that a special interest group advocates, then the group may recruit this person to be placed on the ballot. And then when that person wins, his or her allegiance is going to be to this group that essentially engineered the candidacy. When an interest group or a motivated group of individuals provides the funding and other resources (campaign volunteers, office space, printing needs, etc) that make victory possible, the newly elected official is going to feel compelled to respond with his votes. When the general community then goes to that representative as a collective and expresses how it feels about the particular issue that brought the leader into power, many times that elected official must choose between the best interest of the constituents and the demands of those persons who got him elected. Sadly, when the two groups are at odds, the political leader is more often going to choose the brokers of power, those who were engaged in the campaign process, when making a decision. The everyday voter is pushed aside in the interest of those who are engaged every day in the electoral process. This is not meant to criticize the elected official for the choice that he makes here. Instead, it is a commentary on the state of our electoral system. We have established a power structure in our halls of government that necessitate playing the game, at least to a certain extent, just to stay relevant in the conversations that might benefit our community. If no attention is paid to the special interest groups, a politician might find himself without a seat at the table altogether. But, there are some signs that this emphasis on the will of the powerful groups may be diminishing. It may then become a matter of convincing the general public that their access to their leaders has changed as well.

When we first think about the power brokers who have an influence on the way that votes are cast in our country, perhaps lobbyists come to mind. We imagine these guys in suits sitting in back rooms with cigars and handing over cash and favors to win votes. There is no doubt that lobbyists still hold some sway over political proceedings. In 2011, there were more than 10,000 men and women who are registered as active lobbyists in hopes of persuading Congress and federal agencies to their way of thinking. These include representatives of labor unions, large corporations, health insurance companies, and many others. While this number of bodies is quite impressive, the lobbyist population in our nation's capital has actually decreased over the past several years, more so with every year of the Obama administration. In my state of Tennessee, there are around 240 members registered with the Tennessee Lobbyists Association. Even with some prolific names on their payrolls and the understanding on the part of every industry and professional organization that they must have someone pushing their agenda, their influence on the local level of government is not as overwhelming as you might believe. So, there does seem to be an invitation to return to the table for the average voter. It's just a matter of whether or not we are able to believe this opportunity over the perception anymore.

Before we applaud the diminishing influence that lobbyists have on the decisions that are made at the local level of government, let me be clear in stating that lobbying organizations have a needed role to play in the political discourse and we have much to learn from their members in cultivating political power. Lobbyists are engaged in the process. Politicians listen to lobbyists for many reasons and, in some instances, rightly so.

First, effective lobbyists spend incredible amounts of time drafting, reading, and intimately understanding legislation and do not hesitate to reach out to elected officials. It's their job. Most local elected officials don't have the staff, time, or resources to read and comprehend every piece of legislation that is filed. An effective elected official may ask many lobbyists for the pros and cons of the legislation on which they are working. An engaged legislator always will listen and then verify the information received from a lobbyist.

Second, legislators know that lobbyists have access to tremendous resources for elections and officials must be careful not to vote or act in support of a lobbyist's position just to drive money and votes to their own campaigns and pet projects. It is not the responsibility of the lobbyists to diminish their influence over the political and legislative process. It is up to each and every elected official to do his job of due diligence— acknowledging the financial and people power that lobbyists can swing and then balancing the wishes of the special interests with those of our constituents.

Finally, let us acknowledge that lobbyists offer an effective blueprint to constituents. I want us to view lobbyists with an appropriately proportional role in the local political system, with individual voters feeling empowered and educated to do the same. Let us think about what lobbyists do—get educated on the issues, be persistent in their approach, know the players—and then replicate it.

Members of the constituency have the ability to shift the center of influence in our political system back to the heart of the community, but it won't happen without some effort. Have you ever listened to someone complain about the condition of their neighborhoods or the amount of taxes she pays or the poor education that his grandson is receiving? When they are done, do you then ask them how often they make it to their polling place for elections? Did they volunteer for a candidate? Did they go to the mayor or legislature and demand change? If they are willing to admit the truth, their attendance percentage is probably not very high. And did you know that there are special interest groups that count on low voter turnout? Some people actually make it their business to improve the art of voter suppression. They examine the tactics that will encourage their supporters to make it to the polls while making other voters believe there is no reason to leave the house that day. These people don't want democracy at its finest; they just want to win elections. You know what? Right now, we are letting them. So many potential voters are turned off by politics, but the process evolves on a two-way street. Your action and motion are also required.

We have individuals who simply will not vote, who will not engage in campaigns, and who will not go to the debates and public forums that are sponsored by candidates and elected leaders. For those of you who have been to a town hall meeting of some sort, you know you see the same faces over and over again.

Naturally, our leaders are going to concern themselves with the opinions of those who bothered to show up. These men and women are demonstrating a commitment to the cause and likely will make a difference with their own vote and by influencing others when the next election rolls around. Those individuals cared enough about the election that they came to hear the forum. But, as I mentioned earlier in the chapter, even the influence you garner as someone who shows up at the community center or school cafeteria or local library to express your opinion and hear the thoughts of others will be limited if you are not convincing others who think like you to do the same. Will you have more of an impact than someone who chooses never to vote and shows no desire to engage in the process? Yes, but that relative success may not be good enough.

I will repeat the call for activism throughout this book, and that step into involvement must begin with informed voting. That's it. You cannot be an effective figure in community activism if you do not engage in this fundamental act for which millions have died over the years to earn and preserve. Participation at the voting booth is the best way to make an impact and to set an example for others. You have certainly heard the old saying, "If you don't vote, then you can't complain." It's not, or at least it shouldn't be, a slogan to guilt you into driving to your local elementary school once every couple of years to choose some names off a ballot. Instead, these words should serve as a motto for you as you consider the partnership that you would like to have with the leaders around you.

When you vote, that is your clear signal to elected officials and others of influence that your opinion does have consequences for them and you are someone with whom they should join forces. It is possible to have all ships rising in a seemingly tumultuous political arena. Voters just need to show that they are going to show up and stand up for what they believe even when the stormy waters get a little rough and politicians need to embrace the talents and skills of all men and women present to keep the boat not only afloat, but moving towards calmer and more productive seas. This single act also is powerful in involving others in the cause. You may be surprised by the interest that you get just by letting a friend know you are going to vote after your trip to the grocery store or wearing your "I Voted" sticker when you go to church. You just may convince or remind a few other people to get engaged that day as well.

Regardless of attendance at political events and participation on voting day, there are still going to be large numbers of people who express anger and frustration with a political leader once he is elected. They complain that the person who is supposed to represent their interests seems to know nothing about them. But, if they had attended a debate and realized that this official held views that were counter to their own interests when he was still a candidate, maybe they would have decided to make their voices heard at the election. We need to demand information from our candidates about their stances on issues that matter to us. An informed electorate is a powerful tool and one that will ensure our voice is not overlooked.

So often I have seen other communities making "the news," when the Black community is later only reading the news of economic development, contracts, deals and significant policy decisions. I have fought so hard to get our community to stop reading the news and get involved on the front end to help create the news. I have led and served by this motto, "If you ain't at the table, you're probably on the menu."

Admittedly, this is a vicious cycle to which I am referring. We have people with a long track record of being disenfranchised who understandably choose not to empower themselves with the power of the vote, thinking it will make no difference, and they then continue to be disenfranchised. The loud few will continue to control the debate and the legislation because they are counting on the masses not being engaged. They are counting on the masses not participating in government and simply being asleep at the wheel. Then those who are sleepwalking will get upset because their matters and issues and interests are not being served. Who will you serve if you're an elected official? Those who vote and who come to debates and who are reliably engaged in the political process? Or, will you serve the silent majority?

I am a Democrat along with 80% of Black folks in America and proud of it. But, my loyalty is to my community and what is in the best interest of the members of my community. Over the past twenty years I have seen time and time again candidates of the Democratic Party fail to engage the Black community until four weeks before an election. Then these candidates seek out Black leaders to help them drive out the vote. Often they have no legislative record to prove their commitment to improving our schools, providing jobs and economic development.

On the other hand, the Democratic Party consistently reaches out to Labor, Trial Lawyers, the Gay & Lesbian community and other constituency groups for their support twelve months out of the year. They advocate and push for legislation for the advancement of these interest groups. I am told over and over again that Black people don't vote in local elections and very few contribute politically for statewide elections. This is no excuse for the poor record that Democrats have when it comes to serving the interests of the most loyal constituency group they have.

However, it is up to the Black community and our leaders to demand change. Our Black elected officials have too often failed to demand that Democratic parties across our nation serve the interests of the Black community like they do other constituency groups. I have seen this first hand. Now more than ever, our leaders and our community must stop this vicious cycle of failing to engage the political process and then accepting second-class status as a constituency group of the Democratic Party.

It is when the people, the constituents, decide to engage and be involved at every level, from fundraising to political forums, from get out the vote efforts to reaching out to the candidates in order to find out what their positions are and then telling these candidates what matters to their agenda as voters that you finally will have the people's choice. At some point you must decide to stop the cycle of disengagement. The people must be the ones to decide that they will have an elected official who is their choice, not the choice of a special interest group, not the choice of a loud few, not the choice of the powerful, but rather the choice of the people. It is only at that time when you will have true leadership. Because the leader then must then be responsive to the masses of people that elected her, the majority who are now engaged in the political process, as opposed to a small few that are pulling all of the strings. Will you do your part to make sure that your voice is heard?

Have Our Elected Leaders Made a Difference?

It is difficult to accept the fact that the standard of living for blacks using several different barometers to gauge this standing has not improved with the growth of leadership in an official capacity and, in fact, has gotten worse in some instances. While blacks, or any demographic group for that matter, should never rely solely on government for their personal success in life, you should expect that leaders from your own community should be advocating to make that road smoother.

When considering the political landscape in this country, the situation has never been better for the African American constituency. We are represented in the halls of Congress, state legislatures, city councils, and even the Oval Office in a way never before seen in our nation's history. While we cannot and should not operate under the assumption that having more African American representation in an elected capacity automatically leads to an improved standing for people in the black community, there is an understandable belief that a diverse set of individuals within our elected bodies will work to focus attention on issues that are relevant to African Americans and that speak to the racial disparities that still exist in this country. These policy matters include; job creation, access to health care, education, a pathway to home ownership, and leadership opportunities in both the private and public sectors. So, when it comes to these matters that are so critical to the successful advancement of blacks in our country, has greater political power led to positive change? Surprisingly and sadly, the answer arguably is no, at least not to the degree that should be expected based on the demographic shift in our elected officials over the last two generations.

In the Congressional delegation that is in place as I write this book, there are forty-two black members of the House of Representatives, although, unfortunately, no black members in the Senate at this time. There are more than 650 black mayors and they can be found in every state of our union. In my home state of Tennessee, there are seventeen members of the Tennessee General Assembly who are African American and Nashville's Metro Council, on which I currently serve as a councilman-at-large, ten of the forty members who serve this great city are black. And, of course, the election of President Barack Obama was a landmark achievement not only for the African American population but for the progress of civil rights in our country overall as we elected the first black man to lead our country and took command of what many perceive as the most powerful office in the world. While representation in all areas of government still do not reflect the strength in numbers of the African American population in this country, we certainly have more seats at the table than at any point in our history.

To further this point, we must examine the number of black elected officials in office in 1960, when the civil rights movement was just beginning to form its crest and segregation and Jim Crow laws were still in the norm in many parts of our country. Do you know how many black members of Congress there were walking the halls in Washington, D.C. in 1960? Four. By 1970, that number had risen to eleven members, but still was only a quarter of the number of African American representatives we have in Congress today. The first African American was not elected as mayor of a city until 1966, when Robert C. Henry was voted to be chief executive of Springfield, Ohio and the election of a black man to lead a major city occurred a year later, also in Ohio, when Carl B. Stokes became mayor of Cleveland. With the exception of Governor P.B.S. Pinchback, who was an African American elected governor of Louisiana during the Reconstruction Era, the first black man was not chosen to lead a state until the election of Virginia Governor Doug Wilder in 1990. In terms of the presidency, who could have imagined a black president in 1960 when men and women of color were still fighting to have a seat on the bus or simply exercise their right to vote? Until recently, the African American population navigated the bureaucracy and politics of our country without much in the way of elected representation.

Without much influence in terms of political power, those who were fighting for civil equality took their efforts to the court system—an institution that claims in its founding tenets to be blind to issues of color, race, or creed. It was within these halls of justice that the fight for fair treatment as promised under the Constitution first gained some formal momentum, in cases like *Brown v. Board of Education* in 1954, which began the slow process of integrating our public schools (an effort that continues to be a struggle even to this day), and *Reynolds v. Sims* a decade later, which affirmed the need for equal population distribution in legislative districts. This latter move increased the African American voice in elections, and made possible the sweeping legislative changes that followed.

Fundamentally, our leaders always knew that the very words of the Constitution offered us the equal opportunity for advancement and success that, in reality, was being denied at every turn. The Commerce Clause, found in Article I of the Constitution, gave the government clear control over the way in which business proprietors handled their stores and hotels and transportation facilities and formed the backbone of what became landmark court decisions regulating interstate businesses and assuring equal access. Written in the wake of the Civil War during Reconstruction efforts, the Fourteenth Amendment included the Due Process Clause and the Equal Protection Clause. Both of these legislative points worked to affirm the equal rights of all people in individual states and therefore formed the basis for substantial court action on the behalf of social justice. Knowing our history is critical to the engagement of the African American population. When we were shut off from the greater American dream, we began the work in our own communities to improve lives and opportunities. When our voice grew collectively stronger, we marched and protested and urged the passage of judicial text that opened doors that were critical to our chances for success. With this foundation in place, we then took to the ballot box to put Jim Crow laws behind us and affirmed our support for those who would do good for our community. Voting mattered then, and it still matters now. Voting can result in an elected body that is both proactive in developing solutions for our communities and also reactive in learning the gifts and skills of their constituents and then engaging them in the process, thereby developing informed citizens who are more likely to vote in the next election. The cyclical effect of voting and answering to the will of the voters always will move in an upward fashion, with the result being everyone being lifted up.

To take a look back at how the black electorate was engaged in the process in generations before us, we see that despite (or maybe because of) the lack of elected leaders advocating on our behalf fifty and sixty years ago, the members of African American communities worked together to achieve progress in areas in which we knew we could not rely on our governing bodies for support. The notion that "it takes a village" first developed out of the collective nature of tribal villages in Africa and popularized in our American culture by then-First Lady Hillary Clinton and her bestselling book of the same name, was very much at play in African American neighborhoods. People knew the needs of the families down the street and worked together to make life better for everyone. When a school or a park needed repair, the leaders in the community gathered people to get the job done. If unemployment numbers went up, business owners found ways to hire their friends and neighbors. Children were encouraged by the elders in the neighborhood to stay in school and be responsible citizens. Families remained intact and operated as a strong unit that offered needed foundation to a sustainable community. Crime rates were not spiraling out of control because we kept each other in check and because everyone felt invested in the safety and the prosperity of the streets around us.

This interest in one another's lives came to make its effect known in very specific ways. The black community was a strong unit that operated under the principle that we were only as strong as our weakest link and that led to the continuous lifting up both of those who would take the lead and those who needed the closest connection to leaders in order to stop from slipping through the cracks. This was the era that groomed many of our great civil rights leaders, as the attitude of perseverance and engagement was prolific in our homes, our schools, and our neighborhood centers of activity. It was not only politicians and other leaders who blossomed out of this environment, but also an amazing generation of teachers, scientists, writers, and others who made their impact felt on the way our community was presented and understood. Without a tight knit support system of neighbors and extended family, I would guess that the levels of educational, professional and civic success attained would not have been nearly as powerful or enduring.

Out of this collective mindset, through which every person was working towards a common goal and offering their talents to the cause, true leaders emerged. They spoke out for better schools and recruited the teachers we needed to make that happen. They walked the streets at night to talk to those children who were hanging out on the corner instead of safely at home preparing for another school day. When efforts were made to disenfranchise black voters, stifle black businesses, or discriminate against black students, the leaders stood with courage and the support of their followers in the neighborhoods to make sure that justice claimed victory. When circumstances changed in the electorate of this country and more of our community leaders had viable opportunities to win at the ballot box, many of us took our leadership to legislative halls and executive residences. In doing so, have we been able to amplify the needs of African Americans and bring about increased positive change? Or, have we simply left our communities behind and become part of the system?

A comparative look at the standing of African Americans in several key areas over time offers us one way to examine the impact of more black elected leaders on our situation at large. Has increased leadership in official positions of power led to better circumstances for African Americans? Have leaders and followers worked together for the common goal of the betterment of all people?

Poverty

If you take a look at the economic situation across the country right now, there are people from every demographic background who are hurting and worried about financial security for their families. But, as has been the case throughout our nation's history, minority groups are disproportionately affected by troublesome economic times. Surely, though, with a more diverse membership in our legislative bodies, some progress has been made. Or has it?

In 1960, 48.1% of blacks in America were living below the poverty level. By 1975, thanks largely to civil rights and social welfare programs that had been enacted by still overwhelmingly white political bodies, that number had dropped to 27.1%. This marked a definite improvement, to be sure. However, I would expect that the exponential growth in black leadership in the past forty years would make for even more gains. As of 2009, though, the poverty rate for African Americans stood at 25.8%-- virtually unchanged from our standing more than thirty-five years ago. The percentage of Americans overall who were living below poverty level in 2009 was 14.2%, meaning that the level of blacks living below poverty was 55% higher than the population in general. This was the first full year of the Obama administration and a time at which a record number of blacks were in elected office, but the numbers for our community continued to be daunting and are still following the same path nearly three years later.

Prison

Much has been written about the astonishing number of African Americans, particularly young black men, who find themselves a part of our criminal justice and prison system at some point in their lives. We know that there are more blacks in prison than walking the beautiful courtyards of our college campuses. We also know that a biased view of certain crimes and unfair sentencing guidelines tend to put black men at even a larger risk of ending up behind bars.

Let's take a moment to look at some of the sobering statistics involving African Americans and the prison system today. Blacks made up 41% of the prison population in 2006. When we look at numbers from just a year later, black men between the ages of thirty and thirty-four were the most likely of any group to be in prison, with eleven percent of that demographic behind bars at any given moment. With the men who are coming up right behind them, it is amazing to think about the fact that one in three black men between the ages of twenty atwenty-nine are somehow under correctional supervision or control. That is simply staggering, but the data does not end there. A black man who turned twenty in 2011 stood a 29% chance of being incarcerated at some point in his life, while a white man born in the same year was only looking at a four percent chance of the same fate. And sadly, one in fifteen African American children currently has at least one parent who is serving time behind bars.

The statistics bear out the fact that the relationship that exists today between the black community and the prison system is not a good one, but certainly the numbers must be better than those we would find from forty or fifty years ago. After all, in the middle of the previous century it was difficult to expect a black person to be tried in front of a jury of his peers or even have his word believed at all. However, the research shows a different story.

If you just look at the high school dropout population in 1960, a group that would seem more likely than others to become susceptible to criminal activity, among this demographic black men were incarcerated at a rate of only 1.4%. By the year 2000, this same subset of the African American population was ending up in a prison cell at a rate of 25.1%. That exponential rise in our prison population is nothing less than shocking. And, it is not just those young men who don't finish high school who are now more likely to spend time in jail. From 1980 to 2000, the percentage of African American men in general who were in prison rose from 0.8% to 9.6%! This explosion in the prison population over the past thirty or forty years is really one of the most stark areas of deterioration in the black community and cause for great concern over ways in which a failure of leadership is letting an entire generation make prison part of its lifestyle.

Unemployment

One of the most common topics of conversation you hear on the campaign trail, for every elected office from the small-town councilman to the president of the United States, is the need for job creation. How are our leaders going to develop opportunities to allow all those who want to work the chance to have employment and how are we going to make sure those jobs are available in a fair and just manner? With the call for jobs being such a loud one for our leaders to hear, no matter if our economy is booming or struggling, surely we would have made some positive changes for our community in this area.

The unemployment rate for blacks in America in 1960 was 10.6% while the overall rate for the country stood at 6.1%. This was during a period in which "Whites Only Apply" signs were not uncommon in the windows of restaurants and retail shops and other more subtle discrimination in the hiring process was accepted and even codified. With our black leaders taking the voices of the community and demanding policy changes regarding job promotion in our country, particularly among minority populations, I would hope that the statistics today would not be so grim.

The unemployment rate for African Americans in the summer of 2012 was 14.4% -- five percent higher than it was at the start of the 1960s. To put this number in a greater context, the unemployment rate for the American population at large as I write this book is now 8.1%. This means that not only is the black unemployment rate significantly higher than it was fifty years ago, but that the disparity between the black population and the people in this country overall has not improved at all.

<u>Single Parenthood</u>

We are all aware of the difficult task that is faced by single mothers in this country. Children who are raised in a home in which both parents are not present are more likely to have behavior problems in school or drop out altogether, grow up in poverty, become another statistic in our prison population, and end up single parents themselves. Are all children raised by one parent destined to such a future? Certainly not. But, the odds for struggles increase greatly.

While our elected officials cannot step in between a teenage girl and her boyfriend and tell them to stop having sex, their efforts in the related areas of education, job creation, and community development can make a difference in the pregnancy rate. If we agree that the family is at the core of any society, than shouldn't a politician who is supposedly working for the general welfare of the people he represents be focused on this all-important structure?

The situation we are facing right now is that 72% of African American babies are brought into this world today by unwed mothers, as compared to 41% of all babies in this country. And, not on an unrelated note, 35.7% of African American children are living below the poverty level. That has ramifications that last well beyond worrying about how to get food on the table for dinner that night. The number of black children not born to a man and woman living in a marriage has skyrocketed over the last fifty years, with only 23% of African Americans born to unwed mothers in 1960. That makes for a three hundred percent increase in single motherhood over the past two generations of women.

At the very least, knowing the financial and emotional ramifications of raising a child without a father, our elected officials should be using their positions of influence to bring light to these numbers and encourage our young people to have children only when they are fully grown and in a relationship that will create a two-parent household for our kids. Why are so many of our leaders afraid to speak out with force on this crucial issue?

I am not trying to say that the news is all bad for African Americans in 2012. The number of black men and women who are graduating from high school and college continues to rise, home ownership among all minority groups is at an all-time high, and black-owned businesses are multiplying in number and influence in our country. These are all points of progress that should be recognized and applauded. And, to the extent that our elected leaders have had an influence on these factors, as they most certainly have, they should be thanked. My goal is not to paint a bleak picture for African Americans in this country. But, I must come back to some of the fundamental issues that are plaguing the black community and wonder where our leaders are in taking the front line in the charge to combat them.

When you look at the disturbing fact that prison and unemployment rates have gone up over the last fifty years and poverty levels have seen very little improvement, you can get the sense that we as African Americans have accepted our plight. Moreover, too many of our leaders who once fought to change the status quo have gone on to be with the Lord or they abandoned the audacity of hope of changing thirty years of increased unemployment, prison population and high school drop-out rates. We are now seeing entire generations of black boys and girls grow up in neighborhoods that show little hope for opportunity and no one is remaining in the community, or at the very least returning on a regular basis, to make sure that they hear and others hear how much they matter.

How could a politician look in the eyes of one of his constituents and tell him that a 15% unemployment rate is acceptable? How can he convince a young boy that the fact he never sees his father won't really matter as he grows into manhood? How can a leader who claims to have the best interest of his community at heart look around and wonder where all the young black men have gone without feeling driven to do something about it? The truth is, if you never bother to spend time in the community and face the people you are asking to follow you, the job is simply easier. If you don't acknowledge the problem, maybe it doesn't really exist.

This lack of connection to constituents happens for a couple of reasons. In some instances, our leaders enter elected office with the best of intentions but realize that playing the political game is the only way to achieve even the smallest level of success and their days become games of compromise and maneuvering through bureaucracy. There are also those leaders who simply choose to separate from the community. They used the voters to achieve the political office that they desired, and then isolated themselves from the realities of the community because the task at hand was simply too large. They will come back around at election time, but don't expect to see too much of them until then.

But the greatest failure of political leadership in our community is the elected official who knows how to win elections and has no clue and/or capacity to govern effectively once elected. This phenomenon contributes more to the demise of our community than any other factor with the exception of historic institutional racism.

Looking at statistics to make the argument that a greater number of African American leaders in official positions have had an adverse effect on the quality of life for blacks in several key areas is one thing, but the thesis becomes much more real when viewed through the lens of individuals who have lost faith in our leadership. Over the next several chapters, I will introduce you to people who have little or no trust in our leaders and do not believe in the possibility of any real change. Each for their own reasons, have become pessimistic of the political process and have a diminished interest in following the rallying cry of any politician who calls for their active involvement in affecting positive change. As you read their stories, I hope you will reflect on the idea that you might see yourself in one of the profiles and gain a better understanding of why people in general, and African Americans specifically, do not trust our elected leaders and certainly do not want to follow them.

Remembering a Different Time

The disconnect that exists between the everyday people who live in our communities and the leaders who are supposed to be representing them has not always existed. In fact, up until recently, the African American population was one of the most mobilized and active groups for social change in our country. When it came time to stand up for a cause, it was just expected that most people would participate and lend their talents and their voice to the effort in any way they could. Now, when calls for social justice are made, is there a new generation of young people who will carry on the mission and get involved? Have we instead reached a point in our community that this collective effort is no longer seen as necessary and every person is simply out for himself? In order to examine that question, I spoke with one of the most respected men I know—a man who has been a leader in the struggle for many years and now laments the lack of young people who are ready to take over.

If you ever have the opportunity to sit down for a conversation with Dr. Albert Berry, you will leave feeling humbled, more knowledgeable, and undoubtedly blessed by the experience. He is a true encyclopedia of civil rights history, not only in Tennessee but throughout the country. He sat at the segregated lunch counters, fought for voters' rights and greater educational access for minorities, and formed partnerships with other pillars in the community to work towards common goals that were better achieved with the strength of a cohesive group. Dr. Berry earned academic success when the odds were against him and has since earned professional respect in his chosen field of education. Among his many contributions to our community is his work as a founding member of 100 Black Men of Middle Tennessee, Inc., a group that fosters the academic and social development of our youth. Dr. Berry's voice is one that must be given serious weight and attention when examining the lack of involvement by our young people in issues that demand a passion to rally around those who are in a position to lead as well as perhaps require fresh leadership from them.

Berry grew up in the segregated neighborhoods of Indianapolis and reached an awareness of the social divisions in the 1940s and 1950s, before there were many federal or state laws in place to ensure equality and fairness among the races. While the South, unfairly or not, is often recognized as the breeding ground for racism and Jim Crow laws, the city of Indianapolis was in fact a stronghold for the Ku Klux Klan after the hate group expanded beyond its origins in Pulaski, Tennessee. Separate water fountains, schools, theater seating, and expectations for opportunity were all a part of Berry's childhood and developed his perspective on our nation.

When I spoke to Dr. Berry about his experiences growing up, he mentioned that he managed to find some instances of integration through his high school athletic program and a city-wide church organization that embraced all participants. But, what stood out in his mind was the subtle ways that segregation was endorsed and promoted in Indiana. The state may not have had atrocious lynchings and outright violence in the streets, but the men (and it was almost entirely men) in power made sure that the races stayed separate. Berry shared that the Indiana General Assembly passed a loophole allowing local school boards the authority to make their own decisions about school integration and Indianapolis passed a law requiring integration at the ninth-grade level only. This meant that, essentially, most of a black student's high school education was spent separated from the white students. Berry recalled that there were teachers with PhDs employed at his school and he asked these men why they were using their extensive education to teach at the high school level. Their response was that these black schools offered the only opportunity for them to teach at all. And, if they could get a position at a black college, the "Negro" high school (as it was called then) actually paid more. After moving to Nashville, Berry found that this disparity in education funding was also prevalent in Tennessee. The presidents of Tennessee State University, Fisk University and other black colleges and universities had to rely on the advocacy of other Tennessee education leaders, such as those in charge of the University of Tennessee system of schools, to hope for fair pay.

Berry's move to Nashville also introduced him to the Southern Educational Compact, which was a coordinated attempt by states in the former confederacy to keep blacks out of the mainstream professional schools. Legislators set up a system through which they would pay young black men and women to attend Meharry or Tuskegee as opposed to medical school at the Universities of Tennessee or Alabama, for instance. It was a backhanded way of seeming to support higher education for the black community but in reality it was intended to sustain the separate but equal doctrine that the Supreme Court's *Brown v. Board of Education* decision in 1954 was meant to knock down.

Berry noted that these efforts continue to this day, with no politician wanting to be the one leader who will stand up and take away these scholarships on the basis of their racial undertones.

Recognizing the need for transformational change to occur within the African American community in Nashville, Dr. Berry and several other illustrious names in Tennessee history joined together to form the Davidson County Independent Party Council. Among those lending their intellect and energy to the project were; Avon Williams, a State Senator and leading civil rights activist, Alexander Looby, a prominent attorney who defended the young students who sat at Nashville lunch counters in protest, Reverend Kelly Miller Smith, the pastor at First Baptist Church, Capitol Hill as well as president of the Nashville NAACP and founder of the Nashville Christian Leadership Council, and many other amazing men and women. They came together to look at voter rights and reinforce in Nashville the landmark changes that were just beginning to occur on the national level through the Civil Rights Act and Voting Rights Act.

These prominent citizens, most of whom were not elected to official titles of power, led me to the heart of my book's content. I wanted to know from Dr. Berry what he thought of my assertion that the people in the black community are disconnected from our leaders and feel no pull to follow them into the next new movement for change. While my assertion is that a lot of the gap has to do with the distance that gets placed between leaders and followers by the political process and the lure of power, Dr. Berry offered a different perspective that is cause for serious reflection. Are there young men and women being groomed today who will form their own Independent Party Council or Leadership Council when needed? If not, why not?

Dr. Berry believes the next generation is not engaged in the political and civil rights process for two connected reasons. First, the men and women who are now filling our college campuses or have recently graduated have a mentality that argues "I want it now or it's not worth having." There is no sense of delayed gratification and results must be instantaneous. We also have many young people who live with an "it's all about me" mentality. There is very little thought given to the needs of the greater community around them. Both of these mindsets are luxuries made possible by the hard work done during the civil rights era of two and three generations ago and we will look at them independently for their effect on the leader-follower relationship.

When Dr. Berry and his fellow protestors showed up and ordered a soda at a segregated lunch counter more than fifty years ago, they did not return to their homes that afternoon having successfully changed the law and the hearts of the city's citizens. Instead, that young generation that sat at Woolworth and on the front seats of buses and walked through unwelcoming school doors did so over and over again, for weeks or months or even years. The efforts to change the ways that blacks were treated and viewed in this country took time, and we had leaders who were willing to stay the course.

Today, our young people are used to instantaneous access to information through the internet, television, or smart phones. They have come of age during a time in which "Google" is now a verb used to gather information. You do not need to wait for the morning paper to arrive on your doorstep. In fact, it seems that newspapers are on their way to becoming obsolete. You now get breaking news reports on 24-hour cable stations and news websites can post an important story an hour before *The New York*

Times is set to go to print with the same details. When you are accustomed to having anything you request at your fingertips in a matter of seconds, it is difficult to be told that your participation is needed in a movement that may take a long commitment before any results are seen. The generations that follow those who led the pivotal movements of the 1940s, 1950s, and 1960s have lost their patience and need for endurance.

It is not only instantaneous information that we now enjoy, but also global communication that can be transmitted in the blink of an eye. You can now chat with someone on the other side of the world through your computer, a text message offers quick and relevant information much faster than a phone call or even an email, and Facebook is facilitating discussions with people we haven't seen in decades or perhaps never even met at all. Even our entertainment now comes in an "on demand" format. You can program your television to watch your favorite shows at any time of day or night that you wish, and even fast forward through the commercials. And, the shows that we are watching even wrap themselves up in neat and tidy conclusions within the span of their 30- or 60-minute format. Major problems are quickly solved on network television! If you are tired of flipping through the channels and feel like watching a movie, you can have one streaming through your television screen or laptop in a matter of moments. We even can listen to almost any song in the world by visiting the right websites to download our music. We don't have to wait for anything.

Perhaps this technology offers us one piece in our need to equip the new generation. Just look at how President Obama took advantage of online media and networking to develop his campaign in 2008. He recruited countless new voters and contributors just through being accessible via the means with which young people are most comfortable. And, when the time came to announce his bid for reelection, Obama once again turned to the internet and shared his intentions through a web video. Looking through more of an international lens, the mass protests in Egypt and Libya that spearheaded last year's Arab Spring were orchestrated largely through announcements posted on social websites. One statement on Facebook brought thousands of people to one place to demand change in their government. While we may not need our young people to overthrow their leaders in our country, the idea of having that much passion for justice is inspiring. Maybe our elected officials can take Dr. Berry's assertion concerning the "now" mentality that exists today and reach the disconnected through a medium that offers that instantaneous connection they need. Those politicians who are not taking full advantage of the communication tools that technology affords us need to think about whether or not they are missing an opportunity to ignite a spark in our young people once again.

For many of us over the age of forty, taking advantage of technology and social media is easier said than done. I fully appreciate the effectiveness and power of social media. I just find technology intimidating at times and very foreign. I know that it is critical to communicate with my constituents using Twitter and Facebook. But, I didn't grow up using these media tools and it is hard to teach an old dog new tricks. So, I have to force myself to communicate through social media in order to stay connected to voters and the public in general. In fact, I receive harsh criticism at times from constituents because I don't provide more messages and information through these new tools.

I know that I need to do a better job of employing social media to reach the young generation. It is time to step up and engage. I actually know a few elected officials who refuse to use email and texts. Yes, that is right. In 2012, there are politicians in Nashville who will not use email to allow for communication with their constituents. To refuse to change contributes to the growing gap between leader and young follower.

The idea that today's generation wants it NOW is probably an inevitable byproduct of our progress as a society. The technology that our fine scientists and engineers have created has offered wonderful conveniences and connections over the last decade. I believe, and had the sense that Dr. Berry shares my sentiment, that the "it's all about me" mentality is really the more troubling attribute of our young people and one that forms a substantial barrier to uniting with our leaders for a common cause. When we see ourselves as autonomous entities whose progress and happiness are not tied to the greater well-being of our neighbors and our nation, then the group dynamic that we need to have a successful leader-follower relationship does not stand a chance.

This selfish attitude that unfortunately seems to permeate many in today's generation is a large reason that being a "follower" has taken on such a negative association in their minds. We now have no shortage of young men and women who all want to be the leader and who feel it's a waste of time first to volunteer on behalf of someone else's campaign or to take a low-level research job for a new elected official. This is a dangerous moment in our history because it dismisses the need for a leader-follower relationship and only creates one side of the dynamic. We cannot move forward with this unbalanced relationship. As I've stated throughout the book, a collective effort to move our society forward and make circumstances better for everyone in our communities can only happen if all roles are being fulfilled and respected. Our young people, as well as the seasoned veterans of the political process, need to recognize that they have strengths to offer but there are also areas in which they should defer to others. You may lead when it comes to developing marketing pieces for an upcoming event, but then embrace the role of follower when it is time to deliver the keynote speech. We need to get back to the attitude that prevailed during the Civil Rights movement, when people worked together not for name recognition or to stand out as the leader of a cause, but to reach a collective goal for all people. We have seen it done before. Dr. Berry and his peers have provided the perfect blueprint of unselfish devotion to the cause; we just need to decide to embrace the grunt work and detach from the notion that we all need to be leaders in order to be successful. This current mindset will never work.

Dr. Berry acknowledges that the efforts that he and others of his generation offered during the civil rights era have inadvertently played a role in the selfish attitude that seems to be pronounced today. Black students no longer have to worry about the state-sanctioned and institutionalized racism that permeated our society just forty years ago. With so many avenues and choices now available to them, there does not appear to be an urgent need on the part of young African Americans to speak up and knock down barriers that interfere with their chosen goals in life. Black men and women of the younger generation enjoy the freedom to vote without fear of violence or a poll tax, apply to any school of higher learning that interests them, and appear generally free to pursue their individual goals without restriction. With the "big issues" supposedly solved, many African American teenagers and young adults do not see the need for any collective effort to affect change. They have the luxury of focusing on themselves, believing that all of the problems have been solved or too unaware of their history to realize the severity of the problems that were once in place and that were solved by the concerted and united work of the men and women who preceded them.

This "all about me" mindset carries over into so many facets of the political situation in which we find ourselves as African Americans moving into the future. Why take the time out of my day to wait in line and vote when I could be at work making money or spending time with friends? Why should I show up at a town hall meeting to hear opinions about the new playground that some members in my community want to build when I don't have any kids? Why should I care that so many African Americans are without health insurance when I have a great job that covers me?

If these are the questions that are being asked, then a fundamental shift in their thinking or our approach needs to occur. Let's look at the second option first. Is it the responsibility of elected leaders to show our young people how the political process affects them directly? Perhaps we need to be blatant in explaining the impact that engagement with their leaders can have on their personal happiness or achievement. Even the United States Army is appealing to this sense of "me first" with their campaigns that tout slogans such as "Army of One" and "My Army.com," understanding that their potential recruits want to know what they have to gain personally by joining the military. Maybe our political leaders need to admit that they only will get their followers back, or have them for the first time, if they place their shared goals in the context of how their constituents will benefit.

On the other hand, maybe it is also possible to bring back that sense of community and shared responsibility that was such a cornerstone of the civil rights movement. With a charismatic leader who can communicate the issues and make the young people truly believe in the power of acting as a united and connected force, it still may be possible to mobilize the next generation of activists and politicians and community organizers to continue the fight for social justice that is desperately needed today. During our conversation, Dr. Berry cast doubt on the idea that there are any young people who are being groomed to take over the efforts of a generation that is aging. He is concerned that there are not men and women who are ready to take the mantle from his peers and carry it forward. To see the great successes that you have brought to pass, not only for African Americans but for our country as a whole, and then to have to question whether or not the knowledge and skills that you are willing to pass down will be embraced by the next generation must be a very difficult idea to accept.

I have some experience with trying to get young people engaged in the political process and learned first-hand that we need to explore creative ways to reach these men and women, as they are bombarded with a constant stream of media and social outlets making so many other options besides waiting in line at a polling station more worth their time. In 2003, I spoke with students at Tennessee State University and listened to their concerns about the disparity in amenities when compared to Vanderbilt University, the prestigious private institution that is located just down the road. I urged my audience to get involved in the decisions that were being made on their behalf, and that started with getting registered to vote and having a say in the elected officials who were making the laws and distributing the money in Nashville. If all of the students at Tennessee State became voters in our city, and considering the typical turnout for local elections, they could control the council! Despite what I thought to be a compelling argument for their engagement, my words appeared to ring hollow and the youth turnout remained particularly low in the Metro Council elections of 2007.

The election of President Barack Obama the following year certainly produced a bump in young voter involvement. He has managed to energize our college students and other men and women just reaching adulthood like very few other politicians have done, at least in my lifetime. Beyond that, presidential elections are just viewed as more exciting and "sexy" than local elections. These national contests bring celebrity involvement, attention on such popular programs as *Saturday Night Live* and *The Daily Show*, and just manage to convince the general electorate that the winner in such elections matters more than other lesser-known victors. This truth was reinforced when we tried to get these same young voters who had been so excited in 2008 to go to the polls just two years later and it was a struggle all over again. Without a presidential candidate on the ballot, the interest was not there. As an elected official and also a leader in my state's Democratic Party, I was disheartened by our ability to sustain the momentum ushered in by President Obama.

At that same speech I gave at Tennessee State, I met the SGA president, who was also a party promoter. I was struck by the idea that maybe he could help me make voter registration drives and elections a desired place to be. Before I spoke to the students about their civic duty to vote in local elections, but they probably saw right through me and realized that I had a definite motive of self-interest as I hoped to earn a seat on the Metro Council. My assertion concerning the students' moral obligation was outweighed by the reality that they unfortunately perceived I was just another politician who was saying the right things to get elected. So, the party promoter I had now befriended created an event that featured BBQ and a DJ. While the young people were having a good time at a party, they happened to register to vote at the same time. I made it about a social happening instead of focusing on the issues. When the election itself rolled around, we did the same time across the street from some of the early voting sites. People were drawn to us for the music and food, and decided to go ahead and vote while they were in the proximity anyway. This certainly is not a policy-driven and substantial way to get our students and young professionals to show up at the polls, but it sure offered me an important lesson on the concept that sometimes we have to meet people where they are. If students at TSU or Fisk or Belmont or Vanderbilt are simply introduced to the political process, even if it is done through a filter of free food and entertainment, at least the seed has been planted and hopefully will continue to grow and mature just as these young voters are confronted with more serious issues of the greater community.

The leaders for social justice, such as Dr. Albert Berry, who paved the way for the opportunities that so many of us enjoy today offer us an important perspective on how to craft a meaningful relationship between leaders and followers. Berry is part of a generation that did not hesitate to respond when the need for change was made evident. Sometimes this meant working with elected leaders to promote progress in areas of voting rights, equal treatment under the law, and other legislative matters. Other times, these men and women had to develop their own leadership in order to fight an established system of elected officials who were unwilling to upset the status quo. Either way, the fact that this generation would be involved in the issues that affected the greater community was never in question. We now face a different time in terms of the specific nature of the struggles still facing us and the methods through which we communicate with one another about these issues, but the need for strong leaders to take charge and for passionate followers to lend their voice and talents is still critical. Let us learn what we can from the amazing role models we have been given and not waste their knowledge and insight by failing to become engaged once again. This work must be done by both the elected officials who no longer reach out their constituents and ask for their participation and insight and by young men and women who need to take off their blinders and open their eyes to the roles they must play in the progress of their neighborhood and the nation.

Change for the Next Generation

M elody is getting ready to start her senior year at one of the larger high schools in my home of Nashville. She is enrolled in many honors classes, she plays for the girls' basketball team, and she hopes to attend college next year to study business. In addition to her obvious focus on academics and school activities, Melody works a part-time job at a well-known fast food restaurant to earn a little spending money and save up for a car. She has many of the qualities that would typically mark a future leader for our community, so I was curious to get her perspective on the current dynamics of our political system. How does she see herself fitting into the process, if at all? What impact does she see our elected officials as having on her life? Melody's thoughts on these issues would offer some important insight into what our future holds.

Not to my surprise but still disappointing, Melody does not know the name of her congressman, Nashville's mayor, or even the vice-president of the United States. She did not seem embarrassed by this lack of knowledge, but instead wondered why I would deem it so important. Melody also mentioned that her social studies teacher had been encouraging her and other seniors to register to vote, as she would be turning eighteen in a few months, but she just didn't see the point. I asked her if she would be interested in volunteering for my campaign, as I was intent on engaging young people in my efforts for change, and she still showed no interest. I asked her why she didn't want to get involved. She summarized one of the main contentions of this book when she looked me straight in the eyes and said, "These people put up their signs and get on TV but I don't really think that they care at all. They know nothing about me, my school, or my family. Why should I give them my time? What are they really going to do based on anything I could say?"

Our young men and women are growing up with the idea that their voice does not matter. Their concerns, their struggles, and even their achievements are all brushed aside as irrelevant. What is stunning about this new reality is young people, those from about eighteen to twenty-five years in age, are the ones who were adamant about making sure that what they wanted to say would be heard during the Civil Rights movement. Can you begin to imagine the Freedom Riders, lunch counter protesters, or athletic field integrators without the pivotal force of college students? Now, this same demographic cannot even be convinced to show up and vote in most local elections. What has changed over the last forty years and what can we do to get our young men and women back into active roles for the betterment of our communities and our nation?

The apathy that exists among our young people when it comes to politics is reflected in the statistics concerning voter turnout. In the 2010 midterm elections, the number of voters between the ages of eighteen and twenty-five who came out to the ballot box constituted just 22% of all those who were eligible in that bracket to cast a vote. This low turnout has been in place for more than a decade, but young people turned out in numbers closer to 30% in the 1970s and 1980s when the right to vote among that age group was still new and not taken for granted to the extent that it seems to be today. Still, having less than a third of young people at the peak of participation taking advantage of a right to vote that was earned through blood, sweat, and tears indicates a serious disconnect between our political process and the people who soon will inherit this country with all of its promise and problems.

Think about all of the important issues these young adults will be facing over the next five or ten years—paying student loans, starting a family, looking for health insurance, buying a home, preparing their children for school, searching for full-time employment. They have so much at stake for which effective government can play a critical role but the connection is not being made. We are failing our children in helping them to understand that the relationship with their government should be one that offers a path to greater opportunity and a better life moving forward.

There are several reasons to account for the lack of interest that our teenagers and college students are showing in our political process and leadership. Some of these problems were discussed in an earlier chapter when I shared my insightful conversation with Dr. Albert Berry. These challenges include the perception that the real struggles were already overcome by previous generations who fought for rights at lunch counters and ballot boxes and the luxury that today's generation has in accessing information and solving problems almost instantaneously. But, there are other issues worth mentioning as well and one of the struggles we must face starts in our classrooms with the lack of civics and history education that is occurring at all levels of the curriculum.

While the phrase "those who don't know history are doomed to repeat it" may be passed off as cliché, the merit of the idea holds true. Sadly, the 2010 National Assessment of Academic Progress showed that only 13% of our high school seniors have a proficient knowledge of United States history. If our young people do not understand the strength and the courage and the will to endure that those who came before them had to embody in order just to enjoy basic human rights, then how can they be expected to feel a need to continue the cause? One of the best statements I read coming out of the release of this study was printed here in Tennessee, in the *Kingsport Times News*. The editorial page wrote, "Scores like these demonstrate a dangerous spiritual and cultural discontinuity that must be repaired. While the past is not a perfect guide to the present or the future, it is one of the few we have. A society that does not know where it has been cannot know where it is. It is like an individual suffering amnesia — disoriented." Indeed, we are losing our connection to the past and that is going to hurt our movement into the future.

Elected officials can help to encourage our students' interest in history and current events by playing active roles in our schools. Melody would probably know the names of those who are charged with representing her if they came into her classroom once in a while and talked to the students about the issues of the day. You will find candidates clamoring for photo opportunities with teachers and students as an election rolls near, because everyone wants to be known as a champion for kids and education, but do they return once the race is done? What about the idea of a councilman visiting each school in his district a couple times a year to share anything happening in city government that might be of interest to young people and to hear from the students about what concerns or excites them? Or, how about a state representative inviting high school students into his office and offering a tour of the State Capitol (assuming proximity is not a prohibitive issue) to show these teenagers that the process is alive and vibrant. If these relationships are established at a young age, before the opportunity to vote is even mentioned, the political process will not seem as much of a foreign one to students. Hopefully, the expectation that they will be involved will just be a natural one.

I consider the opportunity I have as an African American elected official who serves countywide to engage young people in the leader-follower dynamic as one of my greatest privileges. I want this new generation to see that there are politicians out there who want to have relationships with their constituents and who value every voice. I am well aware of the fact that the people who have allowed me to serve in the capacity that I do are largely the younger voters and minorities who came out in Nashville in strong numbers to offer me their support. I know the power of these groups. As I already mentioned, they are the same people who fought, gave their lives, and sacrificed so much so that we could pass the Civil Rights Act and the Voting Rights Act in the 1960s. It was young people, white and black, Asian, Hispanic, and others who came together in solidarity for social justice. It was their actions and their leadership and their willingness to stand up that now allows all Americans to be empowered by the vote and engage in our government through democratic means. I am honored that this generation worked on my campaign, contributed financially when they could, and believed in my message of activism within the progressive movement. My challenge now is to find a way for that engagement to extend beyond my individual campaign efforts because, as I mentioned, their level of participation is hardly consistent or strong. I want the same teenagers and college students who knocked on doors for me to believe that they matter to the political process no matter whose name is on the ballot.

I like to think of my interest in promoting this engagement as offering the potential for "the great reward." When you are doing work that extends beyond your own promotion and desires and you are engaged in trying to make a difference within the world around you, the Bible says that you will be rewarded. When you help the poor, when you help the disenfranchised, when you help those who cannot help themselves, your great reward is your heavenly reward. You will not receive your reward on Earth, but you will receive your reward in Heaven. Spiritually, that's great. From a moral perspective, the anticipation of that reward in my eternal home is one that offers a sense of redemption and wonderful peace. I know there is no greater approval and hugs of "job well done" than those that I will one day receive from my Heavenly Father. But, I will admit that I am a flawed human and I hope that I am able to see some benefit to my public life will still residing here in this world.

When you look at politicians or other community leaders, it is no secret that they are human just like anyone else; we know this. And, they all have the same human frailties. We want to be accepted, included, and appreciated. It can be difficult to maintain a belief in the reward of serving the public when a lot of what you have been commissioned to do involves helping those who don't engage, who don't vote, who don't contribute to campaigns, and who don't have the power to be there for you when you need their help in return. As opposed to the powerful individuals and interest groups that are always plugged into campaigns and political maneuvering, the unengaged are also the ones who are the least appreciative because they often don't understand what is being done for them. If you are not aware of the negotiations and rewrites and compromises and frustrating conversations that must take place just for the simplest of legislative measures to pass, then you are quicker to dismiss those in the position of making these laws happen. Maybe it isn't admirable or to be commended, but the honest truth is that it feels good to be noticed. Leaders are just as guilty, and perhaps even more so based on their personality type, of needing the ego stroking and the attention.

Special interest groups know how to let government organizations and elected officials know what they are thinking and what they need. They also know how to communicate effectively, whether truthful or not, the idea that what they are advocating is in the best interest of the community. When no one is engaged and speaking up as a voice of opposition, why should the elected official believe any differently? And, when these advocacy groups also know how to develop personal relationships and demonstrate appreciation, most politicians are going to be susceptible to the attention and praise. I'm not insinuating that the way to gain a politician's favor is through bribes or other illegal means. Just a brief act as simple as saying "thank you" means a lot to a leader who feels that he has been working hard for the cause with no recognition.

Take a look at the many elected officials who, once their time in office has come to an end either by choice or through the force of the ballot box, then began to work for the same interest groups with which they had developed a rapport as a politician.

They now are receiving an earthly reward for cultivating that relationship and this typically comes in the form of a job, an honorary advisory position, or some other capacity that results in compensation. The relationship that was formed between the elected leader and the interest group is one that is based on a track record of delivering on promises and offering mutual benefits. To look at our generation of young people and ask our politicians to develop the same lasting bonds with them even though there may be no apparent reciprocal benefits at the outset is a challenge. When a congressman has finite time to spend courting either interest groups that will reap obvious rewards and recognition or college students who are rarely motivated to vote let alone take active roles in the community, the interest group is going to win the politician's attention nearly every time.

If you want to be a leader who is effective at galvanizing the youth and making them a more substantial factor in political activity moving forward, you must brace yourself for a challenge and keep focused on the ultimate goal of your efforts. You may become discouraged when you realize that they are not engaged, they are not following your lead, they are not coming when asked, and they are not communicating when their input is requested. You will fight so hard to push the boulder up the hill, fighting against special interests and others in power in order to provide for those who do not want to engage in the process. At the end of the day, when you've been beaten and battered, there will be no one there to say "thank you" for your efforts. You probably, at least at first, will not enjoy the sense of satisfaction that comes from getting notes of gratitude for the hard work you put forth on behalf of the next generation that you hope will one day lead by your example. You must remember that striving to engage young voters may come with a delayed sense of accomplishment, but it will happen.

I'm reminded of the story in which Jesus heard the ten lepers who cried out "Jesus heal us" and Jesus healed them. Only one of those lepers came back to thank Jesus for the miracle He had performed in their lives. I would never be so arrogant and misguided as to compare politicians to Jesus, but the story does illustrate the same dynamic of providing leadership to those who don't appreciate the efforts being made on their behalf. More often than not, today's young people are not engaged in the process, they don't follow legislation, and they don't keep up with the daily activities of the government at any level. If any group of people is not monitoring and contributing to the governmental process, then it's almost impossible for members of this group to return and say "we have your back" to those elected officials who have their interests at heart.

If you are planning to run for office or perhaps are already an elected official, there are a few questions you need to ask yourself on a regular basis. Why did I run for this office? Why did I seek this position? Why did I want to become an elected official? This is important because I guarantee that you are going to find yourself in situations in which you will want to say, "If they don't care, why should I? If they're not engaged, why should I engage with them?" You must continue to remind yourself, especially when you are dealing with young people, that it is not about you. It's about them. This is a more difficult task to accomplish when you consider that politicians are in a business that is largely driven by ego. I am asking you to run counter to those natural tendencies so that you can be a true public servant and offer yourself as an example of we hope the next generation will then be inspired to become. We are not going to get high school and college students involved in the process if we do not fundamentally change their perception of the system. As has been discussed throughout this book, it has often been the younger men and women who have blazed the trail for civil rights and community activism. Now, the time has come for us to return the favor for this next group coming up.

So, whether that high school junior whose school play you attended ever says thank-you or the college freshman whose Introduction to Political Science class you visited ever knocks on doors for you or another candidate of her choosing or that class of elementary school kids can even think of a single question to ask when leaving a tour of your office, remember that these choices you are making matter and are resonating somewhere in their minds. Particularly when it comes to the young people, it doesn't matter what they can or cannot do for you as an individual or an elected official. Instead, how can you serve them? Because when you serve the youth, you are serving the entire community in ways that will have ripple effects for years to come. God asks all of us to fight for people who cannot fight for themselves, or maybe just do not know how. Ultimately, if you accept this challenge and embrace the needs of the next generation as your own, you will get your great reward.

Reaching the Disaffected

A s I sit down to write this chapter of the book, the schools in Metro Nashville are preparing to start another year. In just a couple of short weeks, students will fill the halls and reunite with friends before settling in to learn about science, history, and math. Many of these kids will be arriving to their place of learning on a school bus, and the image of one of these trusted vehicles always takes me back to a conversation I had with a bus driver several years ago. I was in the middle of my first campaign for a seat on the Metro Council and was spending a Saturday afternoon walking through neighborhoods and hearing from people who I hoped would soon be my constituents. Among the men and women I met that day was Ruth, and my encounter with her has gone a long way in shaping how I think about my life in public service.

Ruth has been driving Nashville students to and from school for more than twenty years. Before I even knocked on her door, I learned from her neighbors that she was a dedicated worker who loved her job and who knew more about the lives of the kids on her bus than many of their teachers. Her own kids were now grown, so I got the impression that she had taken on a grandmotherly, nurturing role for many young boys and girls who desperately needed another adult in their lives to care about them.

I was anxious to talk to her, as she was someone who obviously was plugged into the community, and hear her insight on what was happening to our neighborhoods and our young people. The problem was—she was not too anxious to speak with me. In fact, she came just short of asking me to leave her street altogether. When I finally convinced her that I truly wanted to learn from her, I began to understand the distrust she had expressed at our moment of introduction.

Ruth told me that she had not received a raise in more than five years. She had not even seen a small token of increased compensation to adjust for the ever-rising cost of living. It was becoming nearly impossible to hold onto the small home in which she had raised her two children because it was hard to make ends meet on a bus driver's salary, especially when you consider that Ruth also cared for a disabled husband who was unable to work much outside of the home. She was not only worried about how she was going to pay the bills for this month, but also what the future held. How would she ever be able to retire? What would happen if she or her husband someday needed more extensive care?

She told me that she used to be politically active, always taking the time to learn about the candidates and even volunteering her time and money when she could. Every election cycle, Ruth shared, she convinced herself that this candidate finally would be the one to make a real difference in the community. After all, the talk by the politicians was always impressive. They would promise to improve schools, invest in job growth, and promote better wages for those who were employed in both the public and private sector. Once several campaigns had come and gone and Ruth saw no change, she came to the conclusion that who was in office really did not matter at all. She admitted to me that she had no intention of voting and saw no difference from one politician to the next, present company included.

Ruth is certainly not alone in her way of thinking. There are thousands of families out there who see their standard of living, the quality of their children's education, and their prospects for the future remain the same year after year. Eventually, they learn to drown out the voices of the candidates who make the claim that somehow their attempt at leadership will be different. Look around at your own neighbors, or maybe within your own home. How many of you have seen your school continue to struggle, your paycheck continue to show the same numbers, and the community around you to continue to show the same lack of attention? Your apathy or downright anger is not without merit, as there certainly is compelling evidence to support the notion that most people do not enjoy or suffer from significant changes to their lifestyle once a different leader is in office. Many people now complain that even the Republicans and Democrats have become too similar to one another in their message, particularly at the local level where one usually must win over a narrowly defined group of voters, that one administration seems to flow right into the next. Are you really going to believe someone who shows a committed interest in dynamic change when history tells a much different story?

When looking to reach voters like Ruth and the millions of other Americans she represents through her skepticism and lack of trust, you must begin by meeting them where they are. If you are a member of a state legislature, no matter if it's in Tennessee or South Dakota or North Carolina, take a detour on your way to the capitol building today and stop off at a bus depot or a construction site. Walk up to someone wearing a uniform that indicates their association with your destination and strike up a conversation. Ask the workers there what they think about their jobs, their pay, and the homes to which they reunite with their families at the end of a long day. And, once you have those answers, ask some follow-up questions. And, please note that I am asking the elected officials to do this—those already in power. We need to start proving through our actions that we do intend to be different than those who preceded us. Go to where the people are and then—slowly—take steps that show your conversations will evolve into tangible and meaningful steps that look to nurture this very tenuous relationship that now exists between a voter and his leader.

Sometimes, these conversations may come with some tough honesty that the person on the other end of the discussion does not want to hear. Ruth or someone like her may approach you and share that she has not had a raise in years despite the grand promises made by other candidates to make things better for the working class folks like her. Your response may have to be that, due to contractual restrictions set forth by her employer or the scope of your power, there is little that you can do about helping her get a well-deserved increase in salary. I truly believe that our constituents are intelligent and want a straightforward answer; even if this means learning that they likely are facing another year without a pay increase. Until we stop acting in a condescending manner towards our voters and promising the moon during campaigns when we know we can never deliver, the people who we need to have as our followers will not get behind us. As a state representative, there is little you can do to influence our negotiations with North Korea. Along those same lines, our president is not likely to address the trash on the local playground that is preventing your kids from having a safe place to play. Be honest about the nature of your position. The voters will appreciate you, and not settle on the conclusion that you just must not care when their initial expectations are not met.

Ruth's story reminds all of us who are interested in pursuing some level of elected public service that we must be aware of who our constituents are and what matters to them. I could have walked down Ruth's street that Saturday touting my extensive credentials with the state Democratic Party, the endorsements I had received from high-profile organizations in the city, my plans to start an afterschool basketball program at the local middle school, or my interest in finally completing a much needed repaving of our main business corridor. None of that, no matter how relevant or well-intentioned, would have meant a thing to Ruth in that moment. She looked at me as yet another politician knocking on her door, and all that mattered to her was that she still did not have a raise. Until that crucial detail in her life changed, elected leaders were all going to look the same to her.

It's not just "everyday voters" like Ruth who are disaffected by politicians and the seemingly endless chorus of endless promises that people hear every campaign season. I coordinated a gathering of influential religious leaders in Nashville to attend a meeting intended to promote dialogue with elected leaders at the local and state level. Our governor was in attendance, as well as many state legislators and members of our Metro Council. Politicians and pastors alike were invited to take to the podium and express their hopes and concerns for the future of our city. As the session reached its conclusion, I quietly congratulated myself for an event that was well-attended and seemed to offer a visible platform for an important group in our community. But, my own feelings of pride were quickly deflated when I was approached by a minister whose respect in Nashville is grounded in decades of service and commitment to the community in which he preaches. He let me know that he would never be attending such an event again. Recognizing the surprise in my reaction, he shared that he had witnessed no appreciable difference from one administration to the next in Tennessee's state and local government. He did not believe that the elected leaders in attendance that day had any greater intention than making sure their photos were taken at the right moment. Here was a man standing before me who had long been a great figure in social justice and activism and he also had become disenchanted with the system. He had decided that it did not matter who was in office—the status quo remained unchanged. So, not only average citizens who easily can feel as if they have no direct access to the halls of power but also community leaders from whom opinions and participation are sought are no longer feeling a connection to the political process.

I will be honest with you and share that I do not know if Ruth voted on the Election Day that arrived just weeks after I spent time with her in her driveway. If her outlook on politicians and the intense disconnect she felt from the promises of leadership were as intense as they came across that day, then I would not be surprised to discover that she did not find her way to a polling booth. I am not naïve; I know it will take more than one conversation to make Ruth find value in the political process again. She has experienced years of perceived neglect as practiced by the men and women who are supposed to arrive at their offices of power with Ruth and other constituents at the forefront of their priorities. I do know that the esteemed pastor who declared his intention to avoid any future gatherings that he viewed only as publicity stunts has held true to his word. He continues to decline invitations to participate in such events. In both instances, those involving working men and women who feel that the politicians are not connected to the issues that matter and powerful community leaders who have decided that a legislative avenue is not one worth pursuing, there is plenty of work involving the changing of hearts and minds that lies ahead if we want to repair our leader-follower relationship.

The Role of the Business Community in Fostering Partnerships

The business community is a necessarily integral component of the progress forward that elected officials and their constituents can take together. Whether the issue is creating jobs in a particular community, providing new books to a struggling school, updating the infrastructure to encourage people to travel through commercial districts with ease, or partnering with local charitable organizations to improve the lives of those around them, business leaders can affect powerful change with their influence and financial clout. While the needs and perspective of those in business should never become of primary importance over the other priorities that require the attention of politicians, who better to offer insight into successful financial management and building responsible growth than an entrepreneur who has proven his abilities with these challenging issues.

When looking specifically at the African American community, the prominence of black-owned businesses has exploded over the past decade. According to the United States Census Bureau, which defines a black-owned business as one in which blacks or African Americans own at least 51 percent or more of the equity, interest, or stock of the business, the number of such businesses increased by 60.5 percent between 2002 and 2007 to 1.9 million. This is more than triple the overall national rate during this same time period, which stood at 18.0 percent. And, these businesses aren't just being created at a fast pace, but they also are quite successful. During this period, the receipts brought in by

black-owned businesses increased by 55.1 percent. As our previous administration encouraged on a regular basis, the African
American entrepreneurs in this country certainly have been doing
their part to stimulate the economy!

With the growing influence of black business owners established and the impact that such private sector leaders can have
on our government officials, I wanted to ask one of our area's top
African American business leaders for his thoughts on the state of
political leadership today. Who does he think is responsible for
developing an improved relationship between leader and follower? I also hoped to learn about his experiences with elected
officials. If business owners are frustrated with the lack of connection they have with politicians, particularly when this relationship is critical to their livelihood, then I would have to imagine
that the feeling would be multiplied for the average citizen who
does not carry any formalized influence.

Don Hardin grew up in Nashville during the 1970s and
1980s and was, along with his brothers, raised by a single mother.
While always encouraged to attend school and receive his di-
ploma, Don never gave much thought to a professional career that
might follow his graduation. His mom never drilled the idea into
his head that he was going to attend college, and the idea of more
education was not really on his radar screen. That is, until one
high school teacher stepped in and encouraged him to take an ex-
tra year of math instead of selecting an easy elective that would
have been the choice of most seniors. This exposure to high-level
critical thinking, combined with a field trip to Tennessee State
University that was offered through the math course to learn
about possible fields of collegiate study, turned this average student into a young man who earned an architectural engineering

degree and who has gone on to build one of the most successful construction businesses in the region. The Don Hardin Group is currently overseeing the diversity business program as well as part of the construction management under Clark Construction out of Washington D.C as they build our city's new convention center, the largest project Nashville has ever seen.

Being in an industry that deals regularly with government regulations in terms of zoning, licensing, and contract bidding, Hardin comes to the table with definite thoughts on the current state of elected leadership and how our politicians are perceived by those of influence in the world of business. He admitted that for most of his career his own opinion of the political process was not, for the most part, a positive one. Hardin pointed to instances in which he had been told to donate to a candidate's campaign and to make sure that he placed the check in the candidate's hand himself. It needed to be well-known that the contribution was being made. Hardin understands that politics necessarily works like this on some level, but he has never felt comfortable with that idea. Recently, though, he has been able to look deeper into the political machinations and appreciates the benefit that pressure from elected officials can apply to a project when used to promote the needs and wants of the entire electorate and not just one leader's self-promotion.

So, how does this successful businessman, who is certainly a leader in his own right, define what he considers to be a strong and effective leader? Hardin offered his definition from the perspective of the business world, and the qualities certainly translate to the political arena as well. His initial response was that a leader treats others like he wants to be treated. This trait speaks to the notion behind this entire book; think about what is good for you in terms of education and health care and employment and remember that your constituents care about these issues as well. Put the same amount of consideration and thought into the people you represent as you do into your own professional progress.

He also stated that a good leader is going to be a voice for others. Are you using your platform to further your own agenda, or are you using the influence you have to make the needs of your community known to the elected body within which you work? And, before that even happens, are you taking the time to listen to your constituents so that you know the voice you are offering is consistent with what the voters in your district need from their government? When you run for elected office, you essentially are asking people to give you the privilege of being their voice in the halls of Congress or in the council meeting room; don't ever let your voice be the only one that is heard.

Finally, Hardin defined a good leader as one who is able to recognize the talents and skills of the people around him and determine how to use each individual in a way that best moves everyone to a common goal. This is such an important point because politicians should want to have an electorate that is engaged and active in bettering their own community. If a retired teacher visits your office on a regular basis to share her concerns about the lack of structure that teenagers have after school, ask her to develop some possible programs and invite her to take a leading role in working with the kids in a way that fits her schedule. When a businessman shows up at a town hall meeting to explain his objections to possible construction of an apartment complex, ask the guy out to lunch and learn about what he would consider to be a better alternative for development. Hardin said that most people are eager to please and be productive contributors to their neighborhoods, but they just don't know how or where to start. Sometimes this involves bringing together a diverse group of people who may enter a challenging situation with preconceived notions of one another to the table, and a leader must get the whole team to buy into the role each one will have to play in order for the effort to be successful.

Through his perspective as a leader in business, Hardin offers an expert opinion on the key roles that both the traditional leader and the equally important follower have to play in their symbiotic relationship. Looking back on his traits of an effective leader, all of them emphasize a person's relationship with others. An elected official should be a voice for his followers, but should not be the only one speaking. In politics, as in business, the proper role of a leader is to empower the followers to embrace their strengths and talents. Mr. Hardin certainly has his own intelligence and work ethic and creativity to thank for the tremendous and well-earned success that he enjoys today, but he also recognizes the crucial role that relationship has played in his efforts. He does not view the person answering the phones or laying the concrete or writing the press material that is intended to win over both the media and the general public as a person who is beneath him in the power structure of his operation. Instead, these men and women may be "following" the roadmap that Hardin has established in his role as leader, but he considers them all equal contributors in the goal for which he is striving. This illustration provides a perfect parallel to my thoughts concerning the dynamic between leaders and followers in the political arena. You should never approach an elected official thinking that his or her participation and ideas are any more important than what you bring to the table. And, if you are in that position of political power, you need to view every person you encounter through the lens of determining how you can work together to improve a common situation. This teamwork, this insistence on getting the best out of every man and woman involved, is a trademark of interpersonal relationships in the business model that we must adopt in our political efforts.

When we are not all operating as a united group with an eye on a shared goal, we will never achieve the optimal conditions for opportunities and achievement for the entire population. Hardin pointed to one glaring example in our city of Nashville that exemplified the breakdown in communication between politicians, the business community, and citizens in the neighborhood. The historic Jefferson Street district in Nashville was once the heart and soul of the black community and one that thrived with businesses and music from the 1940s to 1960s but has since become a stretch of rundown buildings and cracked sidewalks. As Hardin remarked, you could take a brick in 1978, paint your name on it, and place it somewhere on Jefferson Street. If you returned today, that brick would still be there. The neighborhood has not progressed or evolved in more than a generation. In contrast, Hardin pointed out the Green Hills area of Nashville that has turned over and redeveloped multiple times over the same period. In communities such as this one, in which the economic status of its residents is more impressive, the people come together to reinvent themselves in ways that keep the area vibrant and relevant. Is this due to better leadership from the local politicians or the efforts of individuals? Hardin argues that it's a symbiotic relationship that requires participation from both.

On Jefferson Street, many African Americans bought property decades ago and have chosen to hold onto it for one reason or another. In some instances, the land may now be owned by children or grandchildren who live in another part of the country. And, the business leaders and politicians have not found a convincing and effective way to explain the benefits of development. There have been multiple plans put forth over the years, but the current owners seem to think that their property is worth more than what is being offered. Or, for some people this house or closed business may be the only thing that they own and parting with it is a difficult idea to face. Even if one or two properties are developed and look nice, they will not survive because the rest of the surroundings do not create a cohesively welcoming atmosphere. Revitalization of areas like Jefferson Street must be done as a collective effort in order for it to be a success. The community, including its business, political, and professional sectors, must work together.

Along these lines, Hardin sees much promise in the ability for a group of constituents to move forward with their elected leaders when everyone is engaged in developing the steps towards a common goal. And again, he returns to the idea that communication must be the focal point of the relationship. Politicians can hear concerns and ideas for improvement in regards to many issues facing a neighborhood during a town hall meeting or a public hearing, but the next steps aren't necessarily there in turning these ideas into implemented plans. Business leaders who have experience in job growth or building construction or marketing strategies can have valuable roles to play in improving the lives of those who live around them and politicians need to tap into this resource in a way that benefits everyone.

When asked specifically about the thesis of this book concerning the responsibility that our elected leaders have to return to their communities and maintain a strong connection and involvement with the people there, Hardin had a unique take that is so important to note and consider. He did not agree with the notion that politicians should be bound never to leave the neighborhoods from which they were elected—to place such a restriction on them is to go against every natural instinct to desire improvement for the generation that follows. He argued that he should not be punished or criticized for wanting his son to grow up in a better neighborhood and attend schools of a higher quality than he did, and the same freedom should be afforded our politicians. As he said during our discussion, "Do I want the same or worse for my wife and my kid than what I grew up with or do I want to enjoy the life that I've afforded myself? And, a politician or anyone else who has made it in the world is no different. However, we have a responsibility to help others get to where they want to be."

The notion of staying in a bad neighborhood if your hard work and wise decisions have led to more financial security may not appeal to many. Instead, if you choose to leave your community, use that good fortune to carve out a better life and then use your life as an example for others.

Hardin also stressed the importance of the shared responsibility that must exist between a politician and his constituents. The relationship is a two-way street that requires active participation and movement forward by both parties. He used the analogy of a pail of water, saying that a voter can come to his councilman or state representative or congressman and say, "I have filled up my pail halfway and put everything I have into it. Now I need help maybe adding more to the pail and then carrying it." In other words, he believes we cannot approach our elected leaders with open and empty hands and ask for them to fill our needs. It is not an official's job alone to know the desires of his community and meet them. Constituents, or the followers, need to show that they are willing to do their part and work with their leader in achieving the goal that they hopefully all share.

While perhaps being taken as a dose of tough love, Hardin thinks that the men and women in a community who are angered by a politician's perceived lack of involvement or interest first must look at what they are doing to better their own circumstances. He shared with me that we all have an equal shot at financial security and thriving communities, but that these achievements require discipline and hard work. He points to his own background as a child growing up in a rough neighborhood and attending a school that did not have a high percentage of graduates, let alone students who went on to attend college. There were other students in his class who made different choices or perhaps did not listen to that one teacher who encouraged them, and their life took a path that didn't find as much success along the way. So, while Hardin agrees with the principle that leaders should be responsive to the needs of the people they serve and work to lift up everyone, he wants everyone to be proactive in bringing their abilities and knowledge to the table.

Do you have a business plan to show your councilman? When you tell your state representative that your school is failing, can you point to the PTA meetings that you've attended and the discussions you've had with the teachers to make things better? If you are upset about the level of crime on your block, have you reached out to other residents and discussed how you can band together to make your street safer? Before you complain to your congressman about the unemployment rate and the difficulty you personally have had in getting a job, have you spent eight hours a day for a month looking for work and considered jobs that perhaps would not be your first choice? These are just a few examples of questions that Hardin wants constituents to ask of themselves before placing the entire burden on a leader who seems disconnected from the process.

Hardin also warns us to remember that we may not know all that our leaders are doing behind the scenes to help constituents. There may be clear instances in which it is obvious that politicians just say what is needed to get elected and then completely disconnect from voters until the next campaign, but maybe there are times that work is quietly being done without the media's attention. Yes, we do need to see proof that our leaders are responsive to our concerns about the large-picture issues, such as quality schools and health care, and they should not continue to have the trust and support of voters if these issues are not being discussed. At the same time, also consider the possibility that individuals or families are being helped in ways that we never know. Hardin asks for that willingness on the part of voters to give their leaders the benefit of the doubt before concluding that all politicians are self-serving and ineffectual.

When we are looking for ways to improve the relationship and the connection that exists between an elected leader and the voters who are being asked to follow him, it is helpful to ask someone who manages such relationships well in his own professional setting to view the problem through his particular lens. By sitting down and learning from Don Hardin about how he views the nature of the leader-follower dynamic in general, we can apply some of the lessons to the political world. In both business and politics, communication between all participants is critical. We must know the interests and strengths and biases of all parties involved. There also must be the ability on the part of the leader to recognize the strengths that exist among the individuals in his district and to assign roles of action accordingly and willingness on the part of the people to accept their roles and become active participants in the process. Finally, the same principles of discipline and hard work that create success in the business world can lead to improvements in our communities as well. Be aggressive in demanding what you need as constituents and show your elected leaders that you have done the research to know that your plans are viable ones.

Even though there are distinctions between what makes a plan work in the private sector and the steps that must take place when bringing an issue before the government bureaucracy, there are just as many similarities to the process and I thank Don Hardin for bringing his knowledge and perspective to my development of a plan to bridge the current gap between leaders and followers in the political world.

My Call to Action

The pages of this book have detailed what may seem to be a rather dire situation concerning the state of leadership as assumed by African American politicians. The disconnect that exists between our elected officials and the people they have been charged to serve has led to declining conditions in our communities, our businesses, and our sense of civic engagement. Right now, as I sit and write in 2012, less than twenty percent of registered African American voters went to the polls to elect our mayor, vice mayor, and our Metro council in our most recent election. When you include African Americans who are not registered voters, you can conclude that all but one to five percent of African Americans chose not to engage in the process. The masses of black citizens are not following the political leaders who have a hold on the official power in our county, and this trend holds true in elections across the country. I did not decide to publish my thesis, however, with the intention of simply sounding an alarm and telling people how bad things are. Instead, I want to use my work as a catalyst for change concerning how African American leaders view themselves and how their position is viewed by others. I want to re-establish that connection that once made strong voices in the African American community a force that improved schools and employment numbers and social justice. So, I now lay out my call to action, not just for the elected officials but for the men and women who are being asked to follow.

First, let me set the stage for you and demonstrate the truth that African Americans are already engaged in a successful, longstanding leader-follower dynamic that has been in place for generations and continues to be a solid foundation in most of our communities. If you look to our religious leaders, the partnerships are there. African Americans trust their pastors and clerics and figures in their spiritual life, and believe that they are valued members of the relationship as well. If you have ever attended a church service at a predominantly black church on a Sunday morning, you know that it is not just one person speaking to a quiet congregation from the pulpit. There is singing and praising and beautiful fellowship that occurs in every square inch of that sanctuary. African Americans have an attendance record at houses of worship that is significantly higher than those of most other demographic groups. The relationship is important and both leaders and followers know their roles and work together to create an electric dynamic. Right now, these religious leaders and the relationships they offer are more trusted than the elected officials in the political arena and we must learn from the first to bridge the gap in the second. Why is it that when we leave the pulpit and head to the halls of Congress, we lose the leader-follower relationship?

I'll begin by detailing how I believe one becomes a true leader while holding an elected title. You must start with a true desire to serve the ones you lead. Are you entering the political arena with a sense of service, or is another factor motivating your efforts?

It is good for people to get involved in politics; it is even better when these same men and women who win elections are then engaged with the actual process of government. But, why do these people want to have a "State Senator" or "Mayor" or "Congressman" as the title they receive from the public and the media? Many times, unfortunately, it's for self-interest. They want to see their names on buttons and bumper stickers. They like what being an elected official implies about who they are and how important others should find them to be. When being a leader is all about appearances and showmanship, the people back in your district will not be fooled for long.

How can you tell that a politician is not connected to the people once he has claimed victory at the ballot box? This person doesn't return phone calls or e-mails and doesn't go back to the schools that were used as a compelling backdrop in campaign photographs. These so-called leaders do not have an agenda through which they are looking to transform lives, transform communities, and transform families. They really have no intention of advocating for the people they serve because they never gave much thought to what would happen after Election Day.

Many constituents have tuned us out, and I believe their apathy is justified in many instances. People come to realize that we only show up when we have a ribbon-cutting ceremony or a parade, or we have been asked to share in someone's public recognition. If there is a news camera or a reporter there, then our presence can be expected. At least, that is the impression I believe we are giving to the public. But, what happens when the schools are crumbling or there's high crime or there's no access to health care? Do they see us in the community then? Do they see us when there are no television cameras around? Do they see us when there are no newspaper reporters around? You only will achieve true leadership when people see you acting on their behalf when there is no one there to give you credit and there are no press releases to follow.

I believe that our citizens would be much more willing to follow a politician who has a strong background in actual service—working in the community, rallying their neighbors, tutoring or coaching at the local school, helping men and women learn job skills or offering support in the difficult task of raising children. True leadership begins with service that is not compelled out of a desire for more votes. When you actually serve a constituency while expecting nothing in return, when you actually confront issues and challenges and you provide true leadership by affecting positive change, you are making the case that you are a leader who deserves to be followed—because, most likely, you are not achieving your goals alone. You are engaging the people and organizing for a common cause in which you are all invested. When voters are looking for someone to represent them in the halls of Congress, you offer compelling evidence of your ability to make a difference when you have actually been involved on the streets of your neighborhood.

I believe we have it backwards. How many times do we watch someone standing on a stage making beautiful campaign promises but who has never served or delivered quantifiable results to the community whose votes he now needs? You should serve first, and then run for office. Instead of declaring grand statements about what you plan to do, tell the people they should elect you based on your track record of service and what *you have already done*. People will follow you if you have already engaged them and served them and because they have seen what you have done when you weren't seeking office. You cannot just decide to appear and show an interest in your community when the act is one that is for your own benefit or you need to ask the people for their support. You must simply serve out of sincere love for people and the desire to improve their situation or out of frustration with the status quo and because you have the drive to make things different. Service comes first. With that fundamental idea in place, people will follow.

With the priority of service established, is there one area in mind for which you have a driving passion? Where will you make your mark with the effort you put forth for the community? It is best to start with one area that you really want to improve and even transform, whether it is schools, public safety, health care, job creation, neighborhood beautification, or another issue of social justice. When you start with one issue of focus and put all of your energy into making a noticeable change there, your work will be the most effective and the people you are asking to join you in the cause will be confident in your resolve.

There is another way that you can provide service to your constituents, whether you are already elected or not—learn the process. Do you know the steps a proposed piece of legislation must take to get through your city council or state house or Congress? What happens when there is a plot of land that is under consideration for rezoning? What role does the school board have in determining what is actually happening in our classrooms? I would be willing to argue that most candidates who put their name on a ballot to run for elected office have never even attended a municipal hearing or asked to speak at their local council meeting about an issue for which they had a passion. They haven't studied the roles that committees and lobbyists and general bureaucracy play in making change happen and therefore have no clear vision on how to be effective once they are in a position to work in that system. You must know how the system works **before** you ask to be elected. Otherwise, you will be ineffective and behind the curve because you need to take the time after the campaign is over to learn how to be a government official when you should have made sure you knew what to expect before you ever printed that first bumper sticker. You simply wanted to get elected and never gave thought to what might happen on the days that followed. If you are considering a future run for office, start now by becoming an expert on the process of governing and legislating. Study the bills that are before your local government in the current session and then advocate for a piece of legislation that you believe will make a difference in your community. Be in touch with your elected officials regularly so that your voice is heard and meet with your neighbors to let them know what you are learning and doing. By placing yourself into the legislative process before you ever ask for a vote, you will gain important knowledge about how the system works and also show those in your community that you are ready to jump into the bureaucratic structure and make a difference.

You must make sure that you not only know the structure and process of government, but that you know the individuals you are asking to follow you. I walked my community before I ever ran for office. Make no mistake about it—there is a difference between driving through your neighborhood and walking through your neighborhood. When you put your feet on the pavement, you see things that you will never notice driving in a car. You will meet people who are gardening in their front yards or talking with friends on the sidewalk or waiting for their kids at the bus stop. You will see the small points of a pride in a community, such as a beautiful flower bed planted in front of a retirement home or the new business that is employing people who desperately have needed a job for months. You also experience the details that need improvement, like the playground that is littered with trash or that has equipment that is falling apart and the elderly woman who feels trapped in her home because she can no longer drive and her community is not safe for taking a walk. You literally touch the fabric of your neighborhood and its people when you walk and make that connection.

Obviously, depending on the scope of the office for which you are running, you may not be able to walk every street of your constituents. No one running for the United States Senate can be expected to visit every household within the borders of his state. Even the candidate who is running for a district seat in a city the size of Nashville will not know the name of every person in every house. But, you must make the effort to know your constituents to the extent that it is reasonable. Consider the attention you give to a home you may be purchasing. Before you invest any money, you complete a thorough inspection, you walk every inch of every room, you check out the quality of the yard, and you probably take a trip around the entire block to get a sense of who your neighbors would be. You go through a similar process when buying a car. You kick the tires, you look at the engine, and you certainly go for a test drive to gauge the car's strengths and weaknesses. Aren't your neighbors worth just as much attention when you are asking them to commit to a partnership with you for the length of your term in office? An effective leader will know his community and the constituents he is asking to serve. And, he will see his neighbors as people who are joining with him in a shared mission to make society better for everyone.

Let me take the idea of gaining knowledge of your community a step further. Not only should you know the people in your district, but you should have a strong sense of the issues that matter to them. You may walk into a community meeting or spend a Saturday morning going door-to-door to introduce yourself to constituents and do so with your own agenda in mind. You meet with these voters with the intention of explaining to them why your issues of priority should be important to them. But, if you are truly a servant, you have to understand what the people want and desire. Engage your community on more than a surface level. If you are calling neighborhood meetings and nobody comes, start knocking on some doors. Take time out of your schedule to go to churches and mosques and synagogues. Go back into the schools and the small businesses and the local barber shops. When you were running for office, you didn't set up a table in the corner of a room and then wait for the voters to come to you. If you were intent on being successful in your campaign, you went out and made contact with as many people as possible. Don't stop now that you are elected. You will be warmly received when people realize that you are just there to listen and learn from them, and that you are not asking for a vote or a contribution. Your constituents will engage you and tell you what matters to them and, with their support your leadership potential will suddenly reach new heights.

Here is an important point to remember. Any politician who wants to win his race, particularly in local elections, is going to focus time and energy on those voters who have a strong track record of showing up at the polls at every opportunity. Resources are limited in these council-level campaigns, and you need to make sure you reach the people you can expect to be there on

Election Day. These races are not the time to throw open a wide net and hope that a lot of new voters show up to select your name on the ballot. It's understandable that people who are not registered to vote or who have a voter's card somewhere in their home but have rarely bothered to use it will not receive mailings and front porch visits from men and women who are running for Metro Council or other local positions. Therefore, it is the period between elections that is crucial to reach out to the disenfranchised. Take the time to establish those relationships when the pressure of an election is not dictating your schedule and slowly cultivate trust and the belief that their voice matters. This dialogue that occurs between elected officials and their followers, or at least those they hope will choose to follow one day, needs to be ongoing and always evolving. But, let's not forget that it's never just one person who is involved in a productive conversation.

Let us also look at the relationship from the other side and realize that gaining knowledge of constituents and the issues that matter to them must be a partnership that everyone is responsible for maintaining. If you are looking at the men and women who serve as our elected officials and you feel no connection to these people, if you do not want to follow their efforts at leadership, then make sure that they know about your dissatisfaction. If you don't even know the names of the politicians who represent you on your city council or in your state government, find out who they are and how you can reach them. Make your voice heard—it is worthy of their time and attention. These councilmen and representatives and senators were given their offices for the purpose of serving you and leading your community towards a goal that should be for the betterment of everyone involved. If you have no idea what these leaders hold close as their core values and issues, then ask them and demand that they know what is important to you as well.

Some communities are filled with high-maintenance voters. These are the men and women who become the "squeaky wheels" in the offices and on the phone lines and in the email inboxes of every politician who represents them. And, we all know what happens to the squeaky wheel—it gets the grease. These districts are going to have their potholes fixed faster, have newer textbooks in their schools, and have businesses that are thriving. All too often in the African American communities, we are not high-maintenance constituents. We do not show up and speak out at municipal meetings or call our representatives when our needs aren't being met. We just become complacent and assume the status quo is the way things are always going to be. Then, in turn, our elected leaders do not feel the pressure to work hard and use every day they are allowed the privilege of representing the people to make a positive difference on their behalf.

So, I place this challenge to those who are being asked to follow but have given up on the idea that supporting our leaders is going to affect any real change. Give it another chance, and arm yourself with the knowledge that will hold your leaders' feet to the fire. Just like the politicians, you are an important player in the governing process. Learn how it works and how you can use it to the advantage of your community. Read about the different responsibilities of a councilman and a state representative and a United States congressman and the president. While one leader will be the person to contact for building a new community center, you will need to reach out to a completely different office to voice your opinion on standardized testing or welfare reform measures. Find out the steps that proposed legislation must take to become a law. Look up the schedule for the next public hearing on a rezoning bill that includes the school on your street and attend the meeting. Become that squeaky wheel and let your elected leaders know that you are paying attention to their actions, or lack of action, even when it is not campaign season. Even if their efforts initially stem from a fear of not being re-elected, your leaders will become more accountable and respond to your needs and desires if they know you are watching.

While I encourage constituents to be involved and demand a dialogue and a proven track record from the men and women who have been chosen to serve, I return to the idea that it is the job of the leader to make those first steps in the relationship. Yes, voters should call you and come to your office to let you know what they think about the issues of the day, but don't wait for them to make the contact. As I have mentioned throughout this chapter, you need to be fully integrated in the community you want to lead. Remove your "politician" hat and take the time to coach a youth football team, volunteer in a kindergarten classroom, or teach a Sunday school class. Maybe you can just walk door-to-door on a random Saturday afternoon in April, when there is no pressing need to campaign. Continue to be **of** the community, not just **from** the community. As I wrote in the introduction to this book, a leader is guiding others towards a common goal. Look around—are you all moving forward together?

Lastly, I am not asking anyone to reinvent the wheel as we work to improve the relationship that currently exists between leaders and constituents. The framework for the dynamic we need to see is already in place. There are community leaders who haven't earned an official title at the ballot box who are accomplishing great things every day. They serve as the model for what our politicians need to be as elected leaders. If you currently hold an office or hope to run for an elected position in the future, plug in with someone who has their "boots on the ground," so to speak, and learn as much as possible. Take note of how these grassroots organizers connect with people in their neighborhood and inspire them to get involved. Why does a particular minister have a packed sanctuary every Sunday morning? How does the YMCA basketball coach get twenty teenage boys to the gym twice a week instead of engaging in activities that could lead to trouble? Why did your friend down the street get more than a dozen people just from your block to show up in her living room to discuss their concerns over increased crime in the neighborhood? Take notes on what is working in other leader-follower relationships and then apply these success stories to the roles that should ideally exist in the politician-constituent dynamic.

Let's first admit as elected leaders that we do not have the following we need to improve our neighborhoods and make a difference for the common good. And, as constituents, let's decide that we are going to expect more from our politicians and then supply ourselves with the knowledge and the determination to make that happen. If the political landscape of the African American community is reinvigorated and the people are together for a shared purpose, the results will be amazing.

CONCLUSION

It is not acceptable that the lives of African Americans have not changed for the better in several key areas despite the fact that we now have more access to the halls of official power than any time in the history of the United States. Unemployment is still high, the prison population is too great, and poverty levels continue to exist at heartbreaking levels because we now have too many black politicians and not enough black leaders. There are elected men and women with dynamic communication and motivation skills whose influence could be unlimited if plugged in with the people they serve, but instead many officials have simply become more players in the political game. Their talents are being wasted and not being used to change society one community at a time, as they likely would have been two generations ago. It may be that the power of the office became too seductive and a leader is now consumed with his own sense of self-importance or the complicated bureaucracy made the path between leader and follower a twisted and confusing one to maintain, but either way that connection that needs to exist between politician and constituent is no longer there and the consequences are sadly apparent.

As I've admitted time and again throughout the pages of this work, I am the first to admit that the very nature of government creates barriers that must be deconstructed in order for honest and shared efforts between leaders and their followers can occur. There are seemingly countless committee meetings to attend that do not seem to further any productive cause. There are some lobbyists who try and use persuasion and sometimes more unsavory tactics to sway your vote. There is the basic lack of civics education in our classrooms that prevent our students from coming to see government as a functioning entity that is in place to address their needs. There have been too many politicians who have come before you and broken their promises, leaving voters to assume that your word no longer deserves their trust. But, in the end, these are all just excuses that are used to assert that a leader and his followers cannot be partners in today's political process, that the system is irreversibly broken. I refuse to buy into that notion. It's simply not true.

We need to return our focus to fighting for the collective interests that we all share—education, employment, health care, civil rights, just to name a few. We need to feel that we are all part of a large team that is moving forward towards the same end zone. The quarterback has to be in place to make the play calls known and control the ball's movement, but just as important are the wide receivers and offensive lineman and centers without whom the ball would never make it down the field. Wouldn't it be beautiful to see the entire city of Nashville come together in a collective huddle and have its citizens pledge to one another that we all will contribute our unique talents and strengths to moving our communities forward? Voters need to stop watching a television broadcast of a Metro Council meeting or staring at the State Capitol as it stands atop one of Nashville's beautiful hills and focusing on the "us versus them" mentality that unfortunately exists between politicians and the people they serve. Instead, let's shift to the idea of "we" as a united body working together. Then, we finally can allow ourselves to dream big about what this change in attitude could mean for our people and our future.

The African-American community has an amazing tradition of leadership and organization for collective social justice. We have done this before, as the amazing history lessons offered by the Civil Rights movement will attest; we have the power to engage both leaders and followers for the collective good. Our efforts have been at the forefront of some of the most transformative movements in the history of this great nation. We have proven time and again, including during events in which our very lives were threatened, that we know what it takes to bring people together and work towards a greater cause than that of any one individual. Our rich history in this country is an important birthright and one that we should consider a great blessing. The model for success is in place; I am not asking anyone to develop a path to successful leadership with no map to serve as a guide. Look to the abolitionist movement or to school integration or voting rights or inspiring moments of pure community activism and you will find countless examples, stretched over generations, of how leadership is done right. Now it's time for us to claim that mantle and make sure that we keep the momentum moving forward instead of becoming apathetic or even pessimistic about the future and our place in it. All of us are needed. When it comes time for the final verdict to be written about the work that we are doing today, any success that we achieve will not be based on one individual. Our effective leaders will get others to stand with them for a cause and create an environment in which they could disappear and the movement would continue. It needs to be about the group, about who you and I can be together, and not the recognition that we hope to achieve for our individual work.

Please let the words of men like Dr. Albert Berry stay in your hearts and minds as you close the final pages of this book.

The men and women of his generation saw first-hand the powerful impact that a united leader-follower relationship can have on our neighborhoods and our country. They worked towards common goals with persistence, patience, and a sense of a shared destiny that we know is lacking today. With Dr. Berry and his peers ready to pass on their lifetime of knowledge and activism to a new generation of leaders, we need them to feel a sense of confidence and comfort that their legacy is in good hands. Will you move forward from your reading of this book with the promise that you will do your part, whether as a constituent or a community leader or a politician in a position of great elected influence, to restore the relationships that we need to make things better in the days that lie ahead?

I am optimistic that leaders will find a way to regain the trust of their followers and that these followers will demand to be involved and to have their interests matter. I have this faith because we have done it before. It is just that we now must learn to negotiate the relationship in a new environment. When we all lived on the same streets and felt the same sense of exclusion from the official power structure, it was relatively easy to form a united front and recognize the shared needs that we all had. Now, some of us are now a part of the political structure that used to shut us out and necessarily removed from the streets we once shared. That may mean that we all have to work a little harder to communicate and move collectively towards those determined goals, but the potential outcome is more than worth the effort.

This change may need to begin as a movement in which a few politicians choose to genuinely lead even though no one is following, but as relationships are restored and common goals are realized, I am confident it will end with communities that are stronger, more engaged, more knowledgeable, and reaching new heights at every turn. The potential is limitless. Let's get started and make this change happen together.

Inspired by Supreme Court Justice Thurgood Marshall, Maynard chose law as his profession. He earned his Bachelor of Arts in 1989 and Doctor of Jurisprudence in 1993 from Indiana University, Bloomington, Indiana.

Maynard is a leader in the Democratic Party. In 2004, he served as the Tennessee Outreach Director for Senator John Kerry's Presidential campaign, helping register over 41,000 new voters in Davidson County. In 2005, Jerry was selected to serve as the Deputy Chairman of the Tennessee Democratic Party under Chairman Bob Tuke, where he was responsible for the Party's day-to-day operations. In 2006, Maynard served as the Tennessee Outreach Coordinator for Congressman Harold Ford, Jr.'s campaign for U.S. Senate and was elected to the Tennessee Democratic Executive Committee for Senate District 19. In 2008, Maynard was elected to serve on the Democratic National Committee's Standing Committee on Credentials representing President-Elect Barak Obama.

With a great-grandfather, a grandfather and two parents who serve as pastors, Maynard accepted his appointment of Sr. Pastor for Southside Community Church in 2008. In 1998 he also served as the Project Manager for the construction of the new $5.7 million, 2,000 seat church facility, Cathedral of Praise Church, Inc, which his father pastors.

Maynard has served as an Adjunct Professor for Fisk University, Meharry Medical College and Tennessee State University teaching Health Law, Business Law and Ethics.

He has volunteered on the governing boards for the Watkins College of Art Institute, Northwest YMCA, Jefferson Street United Merchants Partnership, Inc. (J.U.M.P.), Cathedral of Praise, Inc. (formerly Pentecostal Tabernacle Church, Inc.), City of Life, C.D.C, and the Living Word Affordable Housing Corporation. In 2004, he helped raise over $70,000 for the Northwest YMCA as chairman of the Major Gifts Fundraising Committee. In 2005, Jerry helped secure nearly $100,000 in funding for J.U.M.P.

Jerry Maynard is married to Teresa Maynard and has two children, a daughter Jamille (20) and a son, Jordan (5).

www.ingramcontent.com/pod-product-compliance
Lightning Source LLC
Chambersburg PA
CBHW072143020426
42334CB00018B/1868